Real Estate
Sales Manager's
Desk Book

Other Books by the Author

How to Finance 100% of Your Real Estate Sales, Prentice-Hall,
1981.

*Thirty-Day Accelerated Training Program for Real Estate Sales
People,* Prentice-Hall, 1979.

Real Estate Sales Manager's Desk Book

Larry L. Sandifar

Prentice-Hall, Inc.
Englewood Cliffs, New Jersey

Prentice-Hall International, Inc., *London*
Prentice-Hall of Australia, Pty. Ltd., *Sydney*
Prentice-Hall of Canada, Ltd., *Toronto*
Prentice-Hall of India Private Ltd., *New Delhi*
Prentice-Hall of Japan, Inc., *Tokyo*
Prentice-Hall of Southeast Asia Pte. Ltd., *Singapore*
Whitehall Books, Ltd., *Wellington, New Zealand*

© 1982 by

Prentice-Hall, Inc.

Englewood Cliffs, N.J.

Library of Congress Cataloging in Publication Data

Sandifar, Larry L.,
  Real estate sales manager's desk book.

  Includes index.
  1. House selling. 2. Real estate business—Management.
3. Sales management. I. Title.
HD1375.S258 1981   333.33′068′8   82-7696
ISBN 0-13-766352-8   AACR2

Printed in the United States of America

Dedication

To Cindy Misner, my business associate and friend. If
we are lucky in life, we have at least one person we can
always turn to, who supports us even during our failures and whose loyalty goes without question. In
Cindy, I have such a person and shall always cherish
our relationship.

How This Book Can
Make Your Office a Success

Real Estate Sales Manager's Desk Book deals with all the essential areas of managing a real estate sales force successfully. You are given a wide range of tested methods, all organized so you can quickly select those which are best suited to your type of operation. The most effective techniques and programs being used today have been combined into one volume for your benefit. Below are just a few of the important ways this book will help you overcome problems and develop a successful real estate sales staff:

• Attracting qualified salespeople is difficult for most sales managers; but, by using the techniques described in this book, such as offering appropriate incentives, training, financing assistance, a professional approach to selling and, in some cases, even a weekly expense draw, one office was able to attract *ten* $20,000+ a year salespeople in *less than six months*. You will discover how other offices have increased their staff as well, without sacrificing the quality of their salespeople.

• A proven formula for judging the potential of applicants.

• How successful offices hold on to their top producers.

• In Chapter Seven, "Writing Advertising that Returns $$$$", you'll discover how to get the most effective use of your advertising dollar, as well as:

- how to design a unique and comprehensive advertising program including signs, direct mail, newspaper, radio, television, and institutional advertising.

- how to change your image through your advertising.

- how to profit from the results of successful advertising campaigns used by both large and small offices from various parts of the country.

- tips on using "attention getters" in your advertising.

- how to direct your advertising at a select group of prospects on any particular listing.
- moving hard-to-sell listings quickly, and for a profit.

• Using supervision and control to keep your salespeople's creativity flowing in a team effort without shutting off the source. Chapter Eleven discusses this problem at length and provides you methods for maintaining control, without limiting the ability of your agents to perform.

• Designing and writing a sales meeting every week is a difficult and time-consuming chore dreaded by most sales managers. Chapter Eleven helps solve this problem by providing you with 52 sales meetings. You are given:

- an entire year of formats for sales meetings that motivate, communicate, train, and increase profits.
- clear objectives for your sales meetings that should fulfill your goals and show how to attain them.
- proven ideas of how to get your salespeople involved in these weekly sessions.

• Outlines of four successful trading programs geared towards various sized real estate offices. You'll see how the programs began, how they overcame the problems they encountered, and how they became a success.

• You'll learn how to start a trading program with as little as $1,000 initial capital, and get experienced advice on what *not* to do in your trading program.

• Chapter Fourteen shows you how to teach your salespeople to use financing to generate sales, and how one sales manager tripled the annual volume of his office by teaching creative and aggressive financing techniques to his salespeople.

• In Chapter Five, you'll learn how successful offices obtain listings, and discover the proven and tested techniques your salespeople can use to double their listing inventory. You'll find out how one sales manager, faced with a listing inventory of only 25 properties, mostly in a low price range, came to me for advice on how to improve his listing situation. Using a combination of selective advertising, canvassing, development of high-powered listing presentations (including a visual aid), and incentives for his salespeople to aggressively solicit listings, his inventory tripled in less than two months and the average listing price rose over $15,000.

• How to *sell* property, not just show it. Chapter Six reveals how multimillion dollar producers get a buyer's signature on an offer to purchase.

Real Estate Sales Manager's Desk Book will show you new techniques for solving other problems, such as:

- new floor duty techniques that increase your percentage of results from incoming calls.
- keeping your salespeople motivated.
- developing an effective orientation program.
- designing a training program that guarantees super salespeople.
- the value of using effective forms, including 15 different forms that will improve communications, record keeping and productivity for your organization.
- compiling a handbook for your salespeople on office policy and standards of operation.
- a review of the areas you should include in your policy handbook.
- time-tested techniques for helping your salespeople reach the level of success they want.
- turning an average salesperson into a top producer with proven motivational management techniques.
- examples of those successful, high-powered techniques in action.

You'll see how one office grew from ten salespeople to one hundred salespeople in less than five years; how another used a nation-wide franchise to achieve success; how a midwest office used systematic canvassing to more than double their listing inventory in just a few short months; and dozens of other examples of how successful offices got that way.

What makes *Real Estate Sales Manager's Desk Book* different from other books on managing a real estate office? What can you gain from reading this book that you can't learn on your own?

First of all, you are provided with *proven* successful management techniques used by many real estate sales managers from all sizes of offices. Not only will you receive the benefit of a wide range of sales experience, you will also have the advantage of learning successful *management* techniques from other successful real estate sales managers. Secondly, you won't get theory or vague concepts in *Real Estate Sales Manager's Desk Book.* This book doesn't side step difficult questions by using philosophy. The next few hundred pages deal in actual solutions to actual problems; solutions that can be implemented by you today, with the assets you presently have available to you. You won't get generalizations. What you *will* get is effective, tested, and proven how-to advice that will lead you to successful, and far more profitable, real estate sales management.

Larry L. Sandifar

Acknowledgments

My deep appreciation goes to those brokers, sales managers and trainers who unselfishly gave of their knowledge, experience and successes so you, the reader, could have the advantage of the most up-to-date sales management techniques available. In particular, credit goes to John Collett, broker; John Semler, broker; John Whalen, broker; Jerry Parks, broker, author, and teacher; and Danny Cox, one of this country's most dynamic and exciting real estate sales motivators and lecturers.

CONTENTS

13

Chapter 5: TEACHING PROVEN AND EFFECTIVE LISTING TECHNIQUES TO DOUBLE YOUR LISTING INVENTORY 85

5-1. Understanding Your Agent's Inability to List, 85. 5-2. Ten Time-Tested Avenues Your Agents Should Be Taking to Secure Listings, 88. 5-3. Implementing a Successful Farm System, 94. 5-4. Putting Together an Effective and Powerful Visual Aid that Puts Professionalism into Your Agents' Listing Presentations, 95. 5-5. Teaching Your Agents to Handle the "How much is it worth?" Question, 98. 5-6. Successful Techniques for Overcoming the Seller's Objections, 99. 5-7. How One Indiana Office Uses Canvassing to Fill the Shelf with Inventory, 105. 5-8. Controlling the Seller Until You Bring Him an Offer, 106.

Chapter 6: DOUBLING YOUR SALESPEOPLE'S COMMISSIONS WITH HIGH-POWERED SHOWING TECHNIQUES 109

6-1. Educating Your Salespeople on the Overall Process to Give Them the Psychological Advantage Over Their Prospects, 110. 6-2. Selecting the Right Home for Viewing, 111. 6-3. Setting Up the Sale While Driving Between Properties, 112. 6-4. Ensuring the Best Mental Attitude While Showing the Home, 114. 6-5. Teaching Your Agents to Sell the Home, Not Just Show It, 114. 6-6. Using Psychological Leverage in Concluding the Tour, 116. 6-7. How Your Salespeople Can Get the Buyer to Ask to Make the Offer, 117. 6-8. High-Powered Closing Techniques that Get the Buyers' Signature on an Offer-to-Purchase, 119. 6-9. Showing Your Agents Why Objections Are Opportunities to Close, 121. 6-10. Two Reasons Why Real Estate Salespeople Fail in Their Attempt to Show Real Estate Successfully, 123.

Chapter 7: WRITING ADVERTISING THAT RETURNS $$$$$ 127

7-1. Pinpointing the Results You Want from Your Advertising Efforts, 128. 7-2. Writing Advertising that Cuts

How to Plan and Control For Successful Real Estate Sales Management

Turning your office into a more successful real estate business is not a matter of having enough money, luck, or time. True, the more of these advantages available to you, the easier it is to increase your success, but even without them you can attain any goal you have set for yourself and your office. No office ever opened its doors and immediately became successful. The broker or sales manager had to plan each step in his or her climb to the top and control the surrounding elements, rather than letting them control his or her success.

As you read Chapter One, consider your present business situation. If you're not happy with your level of success, decide to do something about it, because no one else can. Forget about the methods with which you normally do business and revamp your total thinking concerning the operation of your office. No longer accept the fact that you do something a certain way because that's the way you've always done it. Question each management technique, each advertising program, and the true success and ability of each salesperson. Destiny will not guide your office and your salespeople to success. But *you* can, and you will if you are open-minded and creative enough to lead your staff to new directions.

Now, with no excuses of "this is how we've always worked," let's develop a plan for your office that will ensure the success you want.

1-1. *Setting Realistic Goals for Increased Profits*

Just as your salespeople must have a goal to succeed, you also must have a goal for your office if you are to reach the highest level of success possible. Your goal may be to increase listings, increase the number of closings, increase the number of salespeople, raise the volume produced by each of your salespeople, or establish a new and more aggressive image for your company. Or, all of these may be included in your goals. Before you can reach a certain goal, however, you must first be able to visualize it.

The easiest way to determine your goal is to structure it around your budget and a percentage increase in profit that you would like to see in the upcoming year. Let's assume that next year, your operating budget will be $100,000. Your goal is to also make a $100,000 profit for your office. You now have a total goal of $200,000 that your office must earn in the next twelve months. Before you begin working on that goal, however, you must take a look at expenditures for additional advertising, training, and any capital expenditures that must be made to increase your level of productivity. For ease of computation, we will assume that an additional $40,000 will be required for these areas. Your final goal, then, is $240,000 for the next twelve months.

By breaking this goal down into a monthly goal, we see that your salespeople must earn $20,000 per month for your office. After determining the average office commission earned on each transaction in your area, you can quickly discover the number of closings your office must have each month. If the average selling price of a home in your area is $40,000 and the commission rate is 7 percent, the average commission is $2,800. A normal office share of that commission would be 40 percent, giving your office an average commission of $1,120 into your goal of $20,000 per month. You then find that you must average almost 18 closings per month to be on target.

If you are an average-sized office of ten salespeople, this means that each of your salespeople must close an average of 1.8 transactions per month. As you can see, with the proper guidance, even a mediocre salesperson should be able to help you reach your goal, since any agent not closing two transactions per month cannot survive in the real estate business anyway. Granted, if you do not have a staff of ten salespeople, in order to reach your goal of

$240,000, the number of closings per agent must go up; but, you must also realize that if your office is associated with less than ten salespeople, your cost of operating will not be as great, so you will not need to earn $240,000 to make the profit you want.

You should have other goals besides earning $240,000. Take out a piece of paper and number it 1 through 5. On line 1, write in your income goal for the next twelve months. Lines 2 through 5 should be completed in accordance with the needs of your office and the direction you wish it to take in the next twelve months. Your list should look something like this:

1. $240,000
2. Develop new advertising program
3. Develop new company image
4. Attract three $20,000+ per year salespeople
5. Become the leader in our area in the number of listings.

Your goals may be similar to the ones above or completely different from them. Regardless, it is important that your list contain *only* your five major goals. I've seen sales managers that listed 10, 12, even 18 goals they hoped to reach within the next year. They then spent the year moving from one goal to the other, without really fulfilling any of them. There isn't a sales manager, a corporate executive, or a government official who wouldn't be more successful than he ever imagined possible if each year he could reach five major goals.

1-2. Evaluating Your Present Level of Success

Before you can determine how you are going to get to where you want to be, you first have to determine where you are now. While that may sound obvious, few sales managers actually sit down to evaluate their status among competitors or the community in general. This process does not just involve determining a ranking within the community among real estate offices for number of closings, number of listings and number of salespeople. If you are really to know your own capabilities, you must also evaluate what you have to work with and what has and hasn't worked well for you in the past.

The first area you certainly want to review is why, where, and how you attract your clients. What percentage of your business comes from floor duty calls? Of that business, how much is a result of newspaper advertising, signs, word-of-mouth, or institutional advertising? While these answers may not be readily available, they exist, and are important if you want to get an accurate picture of what makes the telephone ring.

Your second area of concentration should be your salespeople. What was each of their incomes in the past year? What was their percentage of success with listing presentations, showings and closing transactions once they received an offer-to-purchase? How many hours did they devote to their real estate business? Are they professional salespeople, or are they space-takers?

Your office may need additional salespeople or fewer salespeople, or your present staff may need additional training and motivation. Even if the latter is true, only after carefully evaluating each associate can you determine his or her capabilities and, in turn, the capabilities of your firm.

You also want to take a look at your company image. This is the most difficult part of your evaluation process. Naturally, you are prejudiced, and certainly view your office differently than does the public. A quick survey by an outside source, such as an advertising agency or someone not associated with your office who is willing to take such a survey, will give you a much better concept of how you are viewed by the buying public. Until you know what aspects of your advertising program or company image are good and which are not, you are in danger of changing those things that work, rather than those that don't.

1-3. *Eliminating Excess Baggage to Increase Profits and "Growability"*

A successful office must be streamlined and professional. It must be the home of productive, motivated real estate salespeople. Unsuccessful salespeople, who merely occupy desk space, do drain you of profits, regardless of what you might think. Not only do they eat up territory but, more damaging, they have a negative effect on your positive thinkers. Salespeople are among the most easily influenced and fragile individuals in the world. They must constantly be motivated.

I have a friend who has seven beautiful children, one of whom is mentally retarded. I commented to him one day what an advantage it must be to have six healthy children in the family to influence and help his mentally retarded daughter. "No," he replied, "actually, she has a negative influence on the others. It is so much easier for them to pick up her bad habits or poor speech, than for her to pick up their good habits." After years as a sales manager, I realized the same was true of salespeople. It is much easier to drain them of their enthusiasm than to keep them highly motivated. Unproductive salespeople also hurt your public image. People who come into daily contact with them immediately realize that they are not professionals. They soon begin to wonder about the professionalism of your office if this real estate agent is a representative sample.

The fact that they may earn you $4,000, $5,000, or $6,000 a year is misleading, and is certainly the most expensive $6,000 your office has ever earned. The time you must spend with these agents is worth more than the earnings they bring to the office. I'm not suggesting that you set an earnings goal for every salesperson and then terminate them immediately if they fall below that level. Good salespeople have slumps, new salespeople may be slow in developing, and previously unsuccessful real estate agents can be converted to top producers. But, as a successful sales manager, you should know enough about people, particularly real estate salespeople, to know if the potential for future success lies within these individuals. If the ingredients and the desire to succeed are not present, you have an obligation to yourself, your office, and your other associates to sever relationships with the low producer.

Excess baggage inhibits your ability to grow, whether in size, status, or profitability. Streamlining your real estate office involves more than just eliminating unproductive salespeople. Other areas of waste include ineffective handouts, nonproductive advertising, and demands on your time that could be handled easily by a secretary or an outside source.

1-4. Handouts

Every office uses some form of handouts to keep their name before the public. Since everybody uses them, most offices feel compelled to keep up by handing out rulers, calendars, phone book covers, playing cards, key chains, pens, and other noncreative items. While handouts certainly can be effective, few real estate sales managers actually consider whether they are getting their money's worth by using them. If you are going to use this type of handout, work with a local printer who can help you come up with a unique item that will truly make prospects think of you when they need real estate services.

The most productive use of this portion of your advertising budget is the development of written material explaining the services of your office, of real estate professionals in general, and/or what is happening in the market today. The general public is always interested in the real estate market and will remember the expert who communicates with them on a regular basis.

1-5. Advertising

Since man began manufacturing products and offering services, he has experimented to find the most effective means of reaching the public with his product. While hundreds, even thousands, of businesses have developed successful and creative advertising programs, we have just begun to scratch the surface of the marketing potential for our services.

Later in this chapter, and in others, we will discuss some ideas on getting the most from your advertising dollar and putting together the most effective advertising program that your resources allow. For now, our area of concern is to eliminate wasteful and ineffective advertising. Only you, or someone taking a close look at your business, can tell you where these areas are: but in general, let's take a look at how you can measure the success of your advertising.

As with handouts, most managers feel they have to use certain forms of advertising simply because their competitors use them. To some extent this is true, but the key is in creative advertising that gets your *message* across, not just your name. You need not use every media that other real estate offices use, nor to the extent to which they use them. Here are a few ideas that have worked well for other sales managers in reducing advertising costs, while increasing the response:

1-5A. Newspapers

Reduce the size of your daily line ad, and put a small ad in a different section of the paper each day, advertising the number of families you have helped in the past thirty days, or include an energy-saving tip, or your commission rate, etc.

1-5B. Radio

Instead of running two, three, or more spots a day with an advertising message, arrange a two-minute daily message on real estate questions, interest rates, market forecasts, tips on investing, moving, etc., sponsored and preferably presented by you or one of your agents. If presented at the right time of day, this will reach a large share of the market and present your office as the local expert in your field, and not just as another company advertising its services.

1-5C. Institutional Advertising

Phone book covers, matches, theater programs, little league fences, etc., are most often ineffective and a waste of your advertising dollar. To reach the market you want—those interested in buying or selling real estate—use your advertising dollars for moving company handouts, placement in motel lobbies and rooms, billboards, or something creative and individualized, like the real estate office that bought and painted a small moving van for use by their customers. Both sides and the rear of the van carried the office's name, address, and phone number and a huge message that read:

"ANOTHER FAMILY BEING MOVED BY . . ."

1-6. Time Demands

All you have is time and expertise. All your salespeople have is time and expertise. And *time* is the only one of these two assets that is limited. In turn, it is the only real limit on your sales peoples' income and on your income. You can eliminate drains on your precious and valuable time by closely evaluating your duties and determining if someone else, whose time isn't as valuable, could do them as well.

For instance, I never pick up an abstract, order a deed, or deliver an abstract. Your abstract company will be delighted to perform these duties for you as part of their service. My secretary keeps track of all lenders' current interest rates, points, and settlement charges, as well as getting loan pay-offs and legal information from the courthouse for me. I am neither lazy, nor inconsiderate of my secretary. I earn money by selling property and motivating salespeople, not by handling details of a transaction personally.

The same is true for your salespeople. You should encourage them to utilize the services provided by abstract companies, lenders, and attorneys, as well as encouraging your secretarial staff to gather information, make appointments, and do their own leg work. Only obtaining a listing, receiving an offer-to-purchase and closing a transaction puts commission checks in their pockets. It is your responsibility to ensure that as many of their work hours as possible are spent productively reaching these goals.

1-7. Creating a New Image that Guarantees Success

Are you happy with the image your office presents to the public? Do you project a professional, successful image? If the answer to one, or both, of these questions is "No," it's time you took positive steps to change your office image. Even if you are satisfied with how the buying public views your firm, a change is often warranted just to ensure that prospective buyers and sellers do not take you for granted.

One successful agency changes "For Sale" designs every few months. Originally, they were looking for the most recognizable and pleasing design, but the results were so productive they continued to change the signs periodically.

"We found, quite accidentally, that by changing our sign design at six-month intervals, people didn't just automatically drive by our signs without having to give a second thought to which office had the property listed. By making them think about us, through the use of signs that are not automatically recognizable, our sales have increased twenty percent."

Other ways of affecting the image your office reflects include remodeling your building, moving to a more modern facility, designing a new logo, adjusting your commission rate, constructing a more creative advertising program, associating with a national franchise network or becoming a leader in community affairs. One agency of twenty-five salespeople even arranged to lease identical cars with their company name painted on both sides. Each salesperson paid for his or her lease, but because of the arrangements made by the agency, the cost was well below what it would normally be.

Later on we will discuss methods of changing your image through your advertising, but before we go on, here are some tips on the most effective and proven methods of changing your company image.

1-7A. Sign Design, Logos, Stationery, etc.

For a reasonable cost, advertising agencies or graphic arts firms will design these items for you. Often, even your printer will be able to help, and all sign companies offer this service. These people are trained to know how to develop the most effective design, taking color, logo, slogan, and pleasing, yet attention-getting design into consideration. The money you spend here will be returned many times by the additional business a professional image will bring to your office.

1-7B. Remodeling, Building, Choosing a New Facility

Select the services of a proven interior decorator and/or architect when designing your physical changes. Again, these people are trained to know what will succeed.

1-7C. National Franchises

Franchises are available with Century-21, Red Carpet, ERA, Homefinders, Homes for Living, National Multiple List Service and others. While each has its good points and has been successful for many, choose your franchise carefully. Compare the advantages and disadvantages of each of them and consider if the cost will be returned to you several times over.

National advertising, local status and the assistance they can offer you are all very attractive, but they also present you with restrictions that may not make an association worthwhile, unless you can see a large profit increase.

1-7D. Coats, Cars, Briefcases, etc.

Requiring all of your salespeople to drive identical cars, wear the company blazer or to carry a briefcase with your company name and emblem are all excellent ways to gain recognition in your community. To keep your salespeople happy, however, you will have to use your buying power to get a large discount on these items, and many times you will have to share the financial burden they create.

1-7E. *Adjusting Your Commission Rate*

Commission rates have been used for several years as a means of attracting selling prospects. Many companies even make them a part of their office image, such as 1, 3 or 6 percent offices. There is certainly nothing wrong with this, since this country is still based on the free enterprise system that not only allows, but also encourages competitive pricing. My only caution is that you present these reduced commissions in a professional manner that does not alienate your competitors or seem to the public as employing "cut-throat" tactics.

1-8. Making Your Office the Home of a Professional

Consider how an attorney, doctor or educator conducts his business. Do your operation and your people reflect the qualities of these professionals? If your office doesn't, your people won't. And, if your salespeople don't, you won't attract other professionals to your office. The process begins with you. You establish the climate, be it unprofessional or professional.

As a member of the real estate profession, I take great pride in my accomplishments, my business, and in the fact that I provide a very necessary service. A recent survey, however, showed that only automobile salespeople were less trusted than real estate agents. That is a stereotype that is unfounded, but one we have created solely by the image we project. I am embarrassed for my profession when I meet salespeople who do not dress or conduct themselves as professionals. Below is a list of areas where you can improve the professional image of your office:

1-8A. *Advertising*

Never use the word "deal." In conversation or advertising, this single four letter word can do more to damage your image than any other. In auto sales it may be a "deal," but in real estate it is a "transaction." Use advertising copy guide services. They will help you become more creative and professional by providing you headings and copy that have been proven. The cost will only be $4.00 to $5.00 per month.

1-8B. *Dress*

Unless you are in a climate that requires a more casual dress, all male associates should wear coats and ties at all times, even during the summer. The only exception to this is that, when working with farmers, you should be prepared to walk the fences and inspect the outbuildings. Your female associates should also be dressed as would be expected of a professional.

1-8C. *Training*

Besides your in-house training program, encourage your agents to participate in seminars, G.R.I. training and other educational sources.

1-8D. *Automobiles*

Your salespeople's cars should be late models, preferably four-door, and always clean.

1-8E. *Office Policy*

Establish an office policy and handbook, as outlined in Chapter Three. (See Section 3-03.)

1-8F. *Status*

Your salespeople are independent, professional business people, not employees. Treat them with respect and give them as much latitude as possible. The more demands you place on them, the less time and creativity they will have to sell. Your guidelines should be geared to govern them as associates.

1-8G. *Motivation and Leadership*

Your salespeople will be no more professional than you. Neither will they be motivated without your efforts. Besides living under the same rules you place on them, provide motivation through tapes, books, and professional sales meetings.

1-9. Creating a New Image Through Advertising

An important part of establishing a new image is your advertising program. While this aspect alone will not bring you the desired results, you will not accomplish them without it. And, in the end, your advertising program will be what generates phone calls and sales. Your advertising will also greatly determine the effectiveness of your agents when securing listings, since an owner will assume he will receive the same type of advertising exposure you give others. Like it or not, you now have an image with the public that was created through your advertising program. Your goal now is to save the good and discard the bad, while making the public notice you through individualized advertising.

As with financing, selling, or any other aspect of the real estate industry, your success is limited to the creativity of the person responsible for the advertising. Too often, offices have used the same type of advertising for so long, that those responsible now think it is gospel which cannot be altered. If you will take the time to sit down with a quality printer, your newspaper account representative, an advertising specialist, and a radio advertising executive, you will be amazed at what they can do for you. Most of them don't tell you because you don't ask. They can show you examples, local or from other cities; they can give you case histories of results; or they can be very creative and design something just for you. Combine these creative minds with your own ideas and you will find that creating a new image through advertising is relatively easy and probably no more expensive than what you're doing right now.

There are only a few guidelines that must be followed. After these, you can be as creative as you want.

1. *Be Consistent.* Use the same format, logo, etc., in all of your advertising.
2. *Be Professional.* Gimmicks don't work. The buying public is sophisticated and knowledgeable.
3. *Be Quality Conscious.* Your advertising reflects you. Quality costs only a few pennies more. It is really only a matter of selecting the printers, newspapers, radio media, etc., who know how to produce quality material.

The new program you choose may require extensive changes, or just minor alterations. I have seen offices change their logo, run their advertising across the paper instead of vertically, run their ad white on black instead of the normal black on white, develop a new slogan, or just change the position of their ad in the paper, all with very positive results. I have helped others develop new signs, logos, slogans, types of line ads, colors, and radio advertising to create a more aggressive and successful image. How much change you want is up to you and your budget. Those who believe, however, that old, established images are best left untouched and have a positive effect on their clientele, are not remaining competitive. People notice change—they take continuity for granted.

1-10. Improving the Quality of Your Inventory

There is a happy medium between "dogs" and mansions. There is a middle ground between all choice, well-priced listings and listings priced 20 percent over market value. You can't have all high-value or well-priced listings, but if they are not in the majority in your office, you cannot maintain the image you want your office to have. You are better off having your sign in front of five reasonably priced homes in the $30,000 to $40,000 range or higher, than having forty over-priced or dilapidated properties. Much of your image over a long period of comes from your "For Sale" signs. While quantity, then, is important, it can have a detrimental effect in the long run if people begin to notice that your sign is on undesirable property and stays there for several months.

I have a few rules that I maintain when listing property. Except in rare situations for friends, or investment property that will not bear our sign, I adhere to them. I have found that not only have they provided me with good listings and a good income, they have also made my life easier by not causing me to worry about property or problems that I can't control.

1. I refer all low-priced properties to offices that I know handle them. Since they have a history of being successful with these properties, I am doing the seller a favor.

2. I do not take listings that are more than 10 percent over-priced. There are exceptions to this rule, depending on the urgency and circumstances of the seller. But, if you can't get a reduction within seven to ten days, don't take the listing.

3. I am very honest with my sellers. I inform them of what it

will take to market their property, what financing is likely to be involved, what I expect from them and what I will do for them. I do not want to be mentally fatigued by dodging my sellers for months or making excuses. It's much easier and less troublesome to be honest from the start.

While I may not list as many properties as others, my listings sell, my signs look good on them, and I get excellent referrals from my clients. Don't get the wrong impression. I *never* believe in appearing as though I am doing my sellers a favor. I serve my clients, and they are doing me a favor by allowing me to do so, but to be less than honest with them or take on a property that I cannot effectively market is not being of service to them or myself.

You can make all of the excuses you want. In all of my consulting, all of my experience, all of my travels, I have never seen a successful office that handled a large percentage of greatly overpriced or run-down property. They are a drain on your time, energies and public image. Get rid of them. Make every property, regardless of price range, have something going for it and for you.

1-11. *Proven Guidelines for Eliminating Problems that Befall a Growing Office*

Below is a list of pitfalls to be watchful of during a time of growth. They are easy to fall into, harder to get out of. They can also stunt your growth efforts.

1. *Don't* hire salespeople for the sole purpose of enlarging your staff. Be convinced that they have the ability and desire to be productive and represent your office well.

2. *Don't* take listings just for the sake of putting another "For Sale" sign in front of a house. This practice will have a negative effect on your goals for success.

3. *Don't* lose control of your salespeople. Keep them informed, trained, and motivated. Ensure that they follow office policy and that they know they are working in a professional office.

4. *Don't* spend advertising dollars because your competitors do, or because a salesperson tells you one sale will return your advertising dollars. Look for the best use of your advertising budget.

5. *Don't* try to do all of the work yourself. Utilize the abilities

of your secretary and your salespeople, and the services of those with whom you do business and of experts in different fields. You can only concentrate on so many areas, until you are not longer effective in any of them.

6. *Don't* assume that what you are doing is working. Keep records, monitor results, take surveys, and evaluate each program. Prove to yourself that you are using the most effective means possible, whether in training, motivating, selling, or advertising.

1-12. Gauging and Monitoring Your Success

In business, you can never assume that anything does or does not work. Neither can you assume that because something has worked in the past, it will continue to work. To ensure that you are utilizing the most effective methods of training, that your office policies and procedures cultivate a selling climate rather than stifle it, that your advertising is bringing in the most business possible, or that your agents are using their time wisely, you must constantly monitor what you are doing and gauge it against past results.

Compare each salesperson's income before and after your training sessions. (Watch for slippage, an indication that retraining is warranted.) Have they increased, and is the increase due to your training efforts? By comparing the amount of time spent developing their business and the earnings that resulted, was one motivational technique more effective than another? If you keep track of *why* people called and which ad they called on, you can determine the effectiveness of your advertising campaign. How is the real estate industry in your area faring, compared with your office's production? Are you gaining ground, losing ground, maintaining your level, or are the competitors' sales slipping or gaining while yours don't? Multi-list records will give you a good indication of the answers to these questions, and the answers will tell you if the market is down in general or if your overall campaign has been effective.

Your records are not only good indicators, but they will also become your best consultants, since what they tell you will decide what steps need to be taken. Actual proof of what works and what doesn't work is the only evidence you should accept. Assumptions only prove poor business practices.

2

Tested Techniques for Recruiting New Salespeople Who Will Become Top Producers

Regardless of your abilities, regardless of the reputation of your firm or the number of salespeople associated with your office, you must be able to attract and retain million dollar real estate salespeople if you are to succeed. Continuous motivation and thorough training are crucial elements to a successful operation, of course, but the desire for success, the talent for carrying out that success, and the proper attitude must be present in the salespeople you attract, before you can transform them into top producers.

Chapter Two discusses how you can attract and evaluate these individuals, as well as how to sell them on your office as the real estate firm best able to boost their earning potential. We will take a look at how to structure your advertising and how to conduct the interviews. You will also find some tips on how to know if you have a winner and how to look into other industries for potential top-dollar producers.

2-1. Secrets for Attracting Successful Real Estate Salespeople

Attracting successful salespeople to your office is best accomplished by having a reputation of being a successful, people-oriented company. That is the image you must project at all times, and one you must develop if you haven't had it in the past. Before you can succeed with any of the techniques you will find in this chapter, you must first be able to project the image a successful person wants to see in his business home. This doesn't mean you have to handle the most expensive homes in town, or be the largest office. You don't even have to be second, third, or fourth in these areas. You must, however, have an attitude of professionalism, success for your size, and something to offer that other offices don't. Otherwise, you have nothing with which to attract a new salesperson, except for becoming second fiddle, and what good salesperson is going to settle for second when he can have first? In other words, if your association can't be better for a salesperson, you'll never attract and keep the best; only the second best.

The secret, then, is to develop a successful, professional, solid image through your advertising and facility, and make your offer more attractive than the frontrunner's. Chapters One and Seven discuss at length how to reach this first goal, so we will concentrate on the second goal in this chapter. Below is a list of benefits that you can offer a new salesperson in order to make your office his first choice. I have used these incentives to turn a mediocre business into a leader in a relatively short period of time.

1. Larger commission split
2. Bonus after certain volume of sales have been reached
3. Weekly draw
4. Training, motivation and assistance
5. Private office
6. Secretarial support
7. Company paid features such as business cards, multi-list fees, seminars, listing presentations, car allowance
8. Productive floor duty time
9. Professional, cooperative atmosphere
10. Monthly contests with valuable prizes
11. Freedom to operate one's own business as a professional, not as an employee who is limited by company-minded controls
12. A solid public reputation

2-2. How Successful Offices Continually Attract Top Dollar Salespeople

Have you ever wondered what enabled successful companies to continually attract the best salespeople? Or did you accept the excuse that because they are bigger and better known, they got the top producers? Surprisingly, my contacts with top dollar salespeople and a survey I ran recently did not show this as being the reason good salespeople associated with larger offices.

These proven, successful salespeople were attracted to large, successful offices, not because of size or reputation, but because of their impressions compared with other offices they talked to prior to making a decision. When they entered the real estate sales field, they were just more individuals with unproven talents looking for a job. They knew little about real estate and even less about the operation of the real estate offices in their communities. But, when they were interviewed, each felt that the office they selected offered them better opportunities and made them feel that they were among a select few who were good enough to become associated with the company.

When I decided to enter real estate sales as a career, I was twenty-one years old and had never sold anything, except vacuum cleaners for a couple of months when I was seventeen. I knew nothing about real estate, selling, or real estate offices. I took my licensing course and exam because a man I worked with in industry showed me his license and told me you could make a lot of money selling real estate. Since I had a wife, two children, and a $125-a-week job, I decided to get my license.

After giving two months notice to my employer and beginning my courses, I began visiting real estate offices to see who would hire me. I talked to four offices, none of which I had heard of, or knew anything about. Their names came to me through referrals of family and friends. My first four visits went like this:

1. "Gee, it's good to meet you. Charlie told me all about you and I'd sure like to have you aboard." (I never even had a chance to open my mouth to show him I could speak.) Still, I thought maybe my reputation had preceded me, so I kept the offer in mind and, at the encouragement of another friend, I met with another broker.

2. "How much money can I make in real estate?" I asked.
   "A good salesman can make $12,000 his first year. You
   have to go to church though, to work for me. You can get a
   lot of business in church."
   Now, I can think of several reasons to go to chuch, but to do
   so for the sole purpose of getting business seemed a little
   scary. Still, $12,000 a year was almost twice what I was
   making, so I put my second offer in reserve and kept
   searching.

3. Now here I was, in a very plush office, in what was obviously a very successful company. This seemed like the type
   of real estate firm with which I wanted to work. After
   fifteen minutes of questioning by the sales manager, he
   concluded, "If you get your license, stop back and see me
   and we'll talk some more."
   I had two thoughts as I got back into my car. First, I was
   upset that he had stated, "If you get your license. . . ." I
   was *going* to get my license. Second, I had spent fifteen
   minutes telling him about myself and why I was good
   enough to work for his office, but he hadn't spent 30
   seconds telling me why his office would be good for me.

4. Like a beautiful girl on a moonlit night, this sales manager
   swept me off of my feet. At first, we spent very little time
   discussing my abilities. I was given a brief history of the
   company and a list of what it could offer me. I was invited
   back for further discussion, which included a more detailed examination of my background and a briefing of
   what was expected from the salespeople associated with the
   firm. Next, I was invited to lunch with the owner and
   broker after they had checked my references and credit. I
   was then given a personality test, and a meeting was set up
   with myself, the sales manager, and my wife, so she could
   get a better idea of what was involved in a selling career.
   Finally, I was offered a job. My orientation would take
   place while I was waiting to get my license, and while I
   was still with my present employer. I felt that I was one of
   the best salespeople in town because I had become associated with a company that showed me they employed
   the best. I had gone through a tough screening and passed.
   And, even more important, they cared enough to court

me. The sales manager respected me and my ability, and felt I would be an asset to his team. When I asked him how much money I could make my first year, he replied, "As much as you want to make. The only limit on your income will be the amount of effort you put into your real estate business."

Guess which office I joined? The secret is to let the prospective salesperson know that you are the best and that you respect the fact that he also has the potential to be the best.

2-3. Writing Ads that Will Draw a Positive Reponse

Not a day goes by that I don't pick up a paper and see an ad for a licensed real estate salesperson, or an agency offering to help someone get their license. To me, these ads reflect the type of office placing them. Most are uncreative and unprofessional. Seldom will you attract salespeople who are more professional or capable than your ad reflects. If your ad is uncreative and boring, so will be the applicants it attracts. If your ad is powerful, professional, and motivating, so will be the individuals who respond. The majority of ads that appear run something like this:

> "LICENSED REAL ESTATE SALESPEOPLE WANTED— We need two new salespeople. If you are looking for an unlimited income potential, we have an opportunity for you. Competitive commission schedule. Call 555-2222, Ajax Realty. Ask for Mr. Smith."

You can improve on this ad, and your own ads for salespeople, by implementing the same techniques you employ when advertising homes. Consider who you want to reach, what you want your ad to do, and the best method of accomplishing your goal. What would make you respond to an ad? Incorporate that same motivation into your ad for salespeople. To give you an idea of how to write an ad that guarantees you a positive response, I have included some samples that are proven response pullers.

"REAL ESTATE SALESPER-
SON—We have an opportun-
ity for two highly motivated
individuals to enter the most
rewarding and challenging
sales field available. If you
possess the qualities necessary to become a member of
a professional team of salespeople, we can help you earn
an income that cannot be
reached in any other profession. Our associates enjoy
high incomes and so will you
with our comprehensive
training program. Call Mike
Stewart at Village Realtors,
555-9137, to learn more
about what we have to offer
you."

or

"REAL ESTATE CAREER OP-
PORTUNITY—Exciting, chal-
lenging, rewarding. Join the
area's largest seller of
homes. With our compre-
hensive training program,
competitive commission
schedule, and reputation for
providing quality pro-
fessional service, we can
help you enjoy an income
unparalleled in any other
field. Call Mark Sawyer at
Robbins Real Estate, 555-
2323, for a confidential interview."

or

"HAVE YOU EVER CONSID-
ERED REAL ESTATE as a
career? We have an oppor-
tunity for you to become a
member of a professional
staff of successful real estate
associates. We will even help
you obtain your real estate
sales license! No more bos-
ses looking over your shoulder, no more limits on your
income, no more depen-
dence on someone for a
promotion. Call us today and
take your first step towards
independence and security.
Jim Smith, Smith Realty,
555-8888."

2.4. *Tapping Outside Markets for Successful Salespeople*

When recruiting real estate salespeople, much of the emphasis is placed on luring established agents from other offices. This philosophy is somewhat like a person who purchases a used car. He expects the auto to perform better for him than it did for the owner who traded it in because it no longer performed as well as desired. Once in a great while, with the proper repairs, the auto does perform better; but, for the most part, the buyer has purchased someone else's troubles. Sales managers, on the other hand, for some reason expect real estate agents who are unhappy or unsuccessful at one office, to miraculously become top producers in another office. Occasionally, this does happen because of the training and leadership provided, but most often, salespeople who move are not any more successful than they were previously. Your goal, then, is to attract a top producer from another office, which occurs so seldom that you must look to other sources for recruiting individuals who can become successful salespeople.

Of the truly successful real estate salespeople I know, all were successful from the very beginning of their real estate careers. Think about your salespeople who are top producers or million-dollar salespeople with other offices. They weren't successful because of changing offices were they? They came from all walks of life, and were probably very good at what they did prior to entering real estate. Why, then, don't we spend more time developing outside sources?

When I review just a few of the $40,000+ a year salespeople I know, I see a varied background that only has two things in common: the desire to succeed and a proven ability to work with people. My quick list reveals previous occupations that include: a tire store manager, a greenhouse construction contractor, a personnel administrator, a cement salesman, a teacher, a TV repair shop owner, a banker, and a housewife. Almost any field contains people who can become successful real estate agents. The mistake many sales managers make is in waiting for these people to decide, without counsel, to enter the real estate industry, and then attempt to recruit them. Why not get a jump on your competitors by seeking out these potential volume producers? They will not be courted by other offices at the same time, you have an entire community to choose from and, since you put the idea in their heads, when you made them an offer, they most likely won't even consider talking to another office before making a decision.

We have been extremely successful in utilizing this method of building our sales staff. The markets we have tapped for potential real estate salespeople include: insurance, industrial product, and retail sales personnel, educators, and even factory workers. The determining factors are not the individual's knowledge of real estate or selling techniques, but rather, his or her desire to succeed, and the ability to motivate other people.

You still must use sound interview techniques and be selective with those you solicit. You cannot use the shotgun approach of taking anyone who says yes, then hope to get some production from them. You must also be willing to spend time training these individuals, and, in some cases, even help them obtain their licenses. In most states, the process of taking the licensing course and passing the exam will take as much as six months, so you will truly have an investment in your new salesperson. If you have used the techniques described later in this chapter to ensure that he or she possesses the ingredients necessary to become a successful real estate professional, your investment will pay off handsomely. Because of the commitment of your time, expertise, and dollars, however, you cannot afford to be careless in your selection of candidates.

2-5. *Assessing the Benefits Your Office Can Offer New Salespeople*

Earlier we discussed various benefits that you could offer salespeople in order to encourage them to become associated with your office. Now let's take a look at other incentives and how your office and its benefits compare with the competition.

To assess the advantages of being associated with your office as opposed to someone else's, you must first consider the needs of a real estate agent. You must ask yourself, and determine the answers, to three questions before you can structure a package that makes your office the most attractive for a salesperson in search of an office. What are salespeople looking for in an office? Why would someone profit from or enjoy your office more than your competitor's? What have you got to offer that answers the needs of your salespeople? While considering these questions, take a look at areas you control and how they compare with other offices.

2-5A. *Commission Split*

What is the normal commission breakdown in your community? Can you make your schedule more attractive than those of your competitors?

2-5B. *Bonuses*

Do other offices offer bonuses based on volume? Can you structure a bonus system that is neither too easily obtained nor impossible to attain?

2-5C. *Weekly Draw*

We attracted three top salespeople who we could not have otherwise, by providing them a weekly draw against commissions. Can you provide such a draw without reducing incentive?

2-5D. *Training, Motivation, Assistance*

Are other offices providing all of the training and financing assistance salespeople want and need? Can you offer your salespeople more time, attention, and expertise than their present office?

2-5E. *Private Office*

If your facility is designed to allow private offices, this can be a big advantage. Even if it isn't, can you arrange your office in such a manner as to provide maximum privacy for your associates?

2-5F. *Secretarial Support*

Let your salespeople know that the secretaries are there to support them. If they are so successful that sharing a secretary does not provide them enough help, let them know you'll employ enough staff to meet their needs. Not only will access to your secretarial staff allow your salespeople to earn more money, it will also make them feel more important and respected.

2-5G. *Company Paid Services*

The cost of providing certain extra benefits to your salespeople is small compared to the atmosphere and relationship created. A professional, successful office should make it a policy to pay for salespeople's business cards, photos, multilist fees, seminar fees, listing presentations, handouts, and other items used in marketing their services. I know some offices that even pay for their agents' Realtor® fees. These benefits make offices stand out from those that merely allow the agent to occupy desk space.

2-5H. *Productive Floor Duty Time*

By keeping a record of floor duty calls and the productivity of your salespeople from them, you can show a prospective agent that he or she will have floor duty time that generates commissions, and that your rotation allows each agent an equal amount of prime floor time.

2-5I. *Professional, Cooperative Atmosphere*

How can you get ahead of the competition in this area? What can you offer that will be important to the agent that is not offered by all other offices? As I've pointed out and will continue to point out, there are several things you can do to make your office the home of professionals and to develop the atmosphere you want. Policy manuals, communications devices such as: change books, sign books, offer books, showing reports, dress codes, and professional listing presentation aids will help you create this climate.

2-5J. *Monthly Contests*

As incentives to become associated with your office, and to produce, contests can be very effective. Not only do they show the salesperson an opportunity to win too and gain something, they also show the salesperson that you reward your agents. Your contests can be for listings, sales, income, calls made, open houses, or percentage of increase in productivity. We ran one contest that for two weeks paid a cash bonus as soon as a listing was turned into the secretary. Another pitted half of the sales staff against the other half, with the group obtaining the most listings winning a dinner. Contests have included trips, leased cars, cash, or gifts. Handled properly, they create friendly competition, incentive, and generate activity.

2-5K. *Independence*

You can offer a new agent leadership, not control; guidance, not supervision; freedom, not restraints. Look at controls and limitations other offices place on their salespeople and decide how you can eliminate those controls and encourage creativity and productivity.

2-5L. *Reputation*

Some offices have a reputation for handling a particular type of property. Others have an image of securing a majority of the listings, while some offices are well known for their service. Whatever your reputation in the community, show your prospective agent how it will work to his advantage.

2-6. *Ingredients Necessary to Produce a Million Dollar Salesperson*

Salespeople cannot be stereotyped. It is impossible to say this person will earn over $50,000 a year, while that individual will earn under $10,000 a year. Selecting a successful real estate agent cannot be reduced to a simple formula. You can, however, improve your chances of choosing those most likely to succeed by searching for those ingredients that seem to be inherent in all top producers.

When interviewing prospective real estate salespeople, you should have a checklist of "success indicators" to guide you in the selection of top producers. Following is a list of the characteristics most successful real estate agents have in common:

- Financial Need
- Desire to Succeed
- Strong Ego
- Confidence
- Communication Skills

- Goal-Orientation
- Self-Discipline
- Good Motivation
- Past Record of Success (Regardless of Area)
- Ability to Make a Committment
- Energy
- Good Organizational Skills
- Status Consciousness
- Willingness to Learn

Sales managers will often base their judgment of an individual on characteristics that really having nothing to do with selling success. Two of the highest-rated salespeople I know in the real estate industry are also the most unfriendly people I know. No one likes to work with them, and both have few real friends. I also am well acquainted with two real estates salespeople who know literally everyone in town, but seldom earn enough from their real estate sales to support themselves. Today's real estate professional is not a back-patter or just a neat dresser. Having a good personality or knowing a lot of people no longer guarantees success. This is not to say that most good agents are grouches, or that you don't need to know numerous people to succeed in the real estate business. My point is that, traditionally, sales managers have looked for the wrong ingredients in their salespeople and that a variety of other factors go further towards determining the potential of a new agent. Look beyond the exterior shell for true "success indicators."

2-7. *Taking Charge of the Interview*

Controlling an interview with a prospective agent is not much different from controlling the interview with a prospective seller or buyer. If you employ the same techniques, you will be in the driver's seat, rather than just along for the ride. You must be the one to establish the atmosphere and the guidelines. You cannot have the applicant asking all the questions, or feeling that he or she has a job for the asking. The applicant cannot be in the driver's seat.

At the same time, you must court the prospective agent to a certain degree. You want him or her to feel your respect, that you are glad he or she is sitting in front of you, and that you have something to offer that no one else has. Just as you would with a client, impart ideas while extracting the information you need to judge his or her potential. Describe your office, your salespeople, your operation, while you ask about goals, experiences and abilities.

This is your opportunity to make a good first and lasting impression on the prospect. Develop the attitude that your salespeople are carefully selected, and can be proud if they become members of your staff. Because of the standards you set and the training and leadership you provide, they can also be assured of success. As a former Industrial Relations Administrator, I found that to attract top-notch people, I had to offer a top-notch operation. I stressed the benefits our company had to offer, the type of people employed, and the history, as well as the goals, of our company. I made them talk about themselves and their experiences, attitudes, strengths, and weaknesses, not by simply asking them to tell me about themselves, but by describing situations and waiting for their comments.

As with a buyer, if you make your statement or ask a question, an applicant will respond and continue with the thought until he has absolutely nothing else to say.

2-8. Asking Questions that Create a True Picture of Your Applicant's Ability, Personality, and Determination

There are certain questions that you can and should ask an applicant that will show you whether or not the applicant possesses the "success indicators" you need in your salespeople. To be effective, these questions must be presented in a manner that does not appear to be qualifying the applicant, but rather as topics of general interest.

How you phrase these questions is as important as what you ask. Presented properly, the applicant will give you tremendous insight into his internal personality. I have listed some of the questions you should present to your interviewee.

"What are your short-term and long-term goals?"

"What do you feel are your major strengths?" "Weaknesses?"

"How much money do you need to earn? How much do you want to earn?"

"Why would you like to sell real estate?"

"What did you like best about your previous (or present) position?"

"What did you like least about your previous position?"

"How do you like to spend your leisure time? What hobbies do you enjoy?"

"I work most evenings until 8:00 or 9:00 o'clock and show property almost every weekend. Do those hours bother you?"

"What do you believe is important for a salesperson when working with people?"

"Describe yourself to me."

"What gets you excited?"

"One of the most difficult aspects of selling real estate is learning to be self-disciplined. There's no one checking up on you to ensure you are doing the right things. Only your income will tell if you are not pushing yourself."

"What accomplishment are you most proud of"

"How do you plan your day?" "What benefits do you believe short-range and long-range planning can provide?"

2-9. Evaluating Your Applicant's Responses

Knowing what to ask and knowing what you are looking for in the response are two different talents. Few people really know their own ambitions, abilities, strengths, and weaknesses. You must be able to "discover" the true picture of the applicant by looking deeper than just the answer to the questions you ask. For instance, if the applicant blames someone else for the separation from his or her last employer or for a failure, is it the truth, or does this indicate inability to admit to his or her own weaknesses or failures, or that he or she looks for excuses, rather than methods of correcting failures?

Similarly, do the responses indicate confidence, assertiveness, commitment? Does he or she have goals, and possess a willingness to work toward them? Everything applicants tell you, as with clients, must be taken with a grain of salt. It is natural for them to give the response they believe you want and the one that puts them in the best light. You must accept these responses, but attempt to verify them through a review of past accomplishments and experi-

ences. The applicants will provide you with this verification, un-
knowingly, by relating their likes, dislikes, work experience, and
reactions to different situations in the past.

I have already provided you a list of criteria you hope to find
in a new salesperson. Compare this list with your applicant's comments:

Commitment—Is the applicant committed to devoting as many
hours (especially late night and weekend) as necessary to
succeed?

Goal Oriented—Does the applicant have a clearly defined, obtainable goal?

Easily Motivated—What gets him or her excited? What makes
him or her want to win? If someone is complacent, hard to
convince, he or she will not be easily motivated.

Desire and Ability to Succeed—Is the applicant good at his or her
present occupation? Was the applicant a competitive athlete?
Is success important to this individual?

Financial Need or Desire—If your applicant is in poor financial
condition, he or she will probably have neither the ability to
stay on commission nor the ability to manage earnings. But if
the person is financially independent, there will be no incentive to make sales. You are looking for that middle ground,
where the need to earn and the desire to increase earnings are
present, but your salesperson won't starve if he or she doesn't
close a sale the first month.

Communication Skills—If the applicant can't express feelings or
interpret what you say, it is not likely he or she could communicate effectively with clients.

Strong Ego—If a person doesn't like or respect him or herself,
no one else will. Salespeople have to feel that people want to
do business with them and should do business with them
because they are the best.

Energy—Is the prospective agent vibrant, alive? Can the person work long hours without tiring? Activities, hobbies, work
habits, can provide you with insight into his or her stamina.

Self-Discipline—One of the most difficult talents to find in
individuals from industrial environments is self-discipline. If
an individual has this talent, it will show up in the extra effort

he or she exerts, as well as in his or her control of life outside work.

2-10. *Five Key Factors Successful Real Estate Offices Use in Judging Potential*

Not all of the "Success Indicators" must be present for a salesperson to be successful. Many of these traits can be learned, while others can be overshadowed by more outstanding characteristics. As I mentioned earlier, you will pass up excellent salespeople if you don't judge the potential of each applicant individually. You cannot stereotype people or use strict guidelines. Common sense and knowledge of people must be used in making a decision. There are certain factors, however, that experience has shown must be present or obtainable if a salesperson is to be a million-dollar producer. In a discussion with several of the nation's top sales managers, we found a consensus among the group of five factors they used to judge the success potential of new salespeople.

- **The salesperson must be hungry.** An agent must have a need, either to meet obligations or to maintain the lifestyle he or she desires.
- **The salesperson must be able to be motivated.** If he knows it all, or is a pessimist, or too low keyed to get excited about selling, you have no motivational leverage.
- **The salesperson must be success oriented.** To be successful at real estate takes a tremendous amount of drive and hard work. If the deep-seated desire to succeed isn't present, the agent will not devote the time and energies necessary to become a top producer for your firm.
- **The salesperson must be confident.** Asking for business and getting eight out of ten negative responses is more than most people can take. Only a person who is confident of his or her ability can ask a person to buy as often as is necessary to get an offer or listing signed. He or she must be able to take charge.
- **The salesperson must be committed.** If a person's priorities are to spend evenings and weekends with the family, or wants to give real estate sales a whirl, or to have a weekly, guaranteed paycheck, this individual will not succeed in real

estate sales. He or she must be committed to doing whatever it takes to reach his or her goal, and willing to spend less, but more productive and meaningful time with the family.

You cannot develop or teach these five factors. Your applicants either possess them or they don't. If they don't, they will never become productive, successful, real estate salespeople. If they do, they are the road to financial independence.

2-11. Selling Your Prospective Agent on You and Your Office

We have already reviewed the benefits your office can offer a prospective real estate agent. We have also reviewed examples of mistakes many sales managers make when attempting to recruit new salespeople. Now that you have assessed the advantages of being associated with your office as opposed any other, all that is required is for you to present your case to the interviewee. To ensure that you make a good first impression on the applicant, and that you sell him on yourself and your office, employ the following techniques.

- You are the image of the company. Many times you will be the only individual the applicant knows at your office. Your manner must be friendly, professional, and warm. You shouldn't appear stand-offish or eager.

- Don't present the benefits of working with your office as though it were a sales presentation. Instead, present a history of your company and a discussion of how you do business. It is not necessary that you give numbers or boast of successes.

- Being associated with your office requires more than merely possessing a real estate license. Your interest does not mean that the position is automatic. The agent will have to earn your respect and be sold on your operation before receiving an offer to become a member of your team.

- Your salespeople earn high levels of income because you provide them what they need to succeed. Present evidence of what you can do for the applicant, and why the benefits you offer are important, by pointing out that your agents are successful real estate salespeople.

The real estate brokerage business is extremely competitive. Many times, the office that controls the most associates enjoys the highest income. All offices have one thing in common; they depend on their salespeople to produce a majority of their income. Because of this and because of the competitive nature of the business, there is great competition for the agents themselves. This fact has lead many sales managers to get into the numbers game and readily accept any agent who expresses a desire to be associated with their offices. Unfortunately, the old adage that "A person does not appreciate that which he acquires without effort" is true. A "take anyone that applies, without question" attitude will result in prospective agents with potential seeking out another office that places more emphasis on the quality of people it hires. If an agent is proud to be with your office, and had to work to become a member of your staff, he or she will work to maintain this position. By utilizing professional interviewing techniques, you can develop that attitude in your new salespeople and get them on the right path to selling success.

3

Developing an Orientation Program That Instills Success In Your Salespeople

You've attracted a new salesperson to your office. Now what? How do you get him or her off on the right foot?

Let me show you how, unfortunately, eight out of ten offices begin their association with a new agent:

"John, it's so good to have you with us. I'd like for you to meet Sally, our secretary. If you need any typing done or want to know where something is, just ask her; she's a great help.

"Now here's your desk and copies of all our listings. You're on floor duty for the next three hours. If you need anything, just let me know. I'm really looking forward to great things from you, John. Good luck."

One month later, John still hasn't made any sales, and his sales manager can't figure out why. He looked so good when he first started.

3-1. Reaping the Benefits of an Effective Orientation Program

John's failure to be productive wasn't his fault; it was the fault of his sales manager. Eighty percent of all salespeople lose the most productive time of their careers due to sales managers' failing to get them selling within the first week by giving them informative and motivating orientation programs. While you accept many aspects of selling real estate as routine, a newcomer to your office or the real estate industry is completely lost.

As I mentioned earlier, I began my career in real estate when I was twenty-one years old, thus I knew nothing about real estate; I didn't even own my own home, and I had sold very little before. Before I ever thought about selling, I spent one full week in an orientation program. On April 1, I was ready to start selling. By May 1 I had sold seven homes, had two listings that sold, and had listed three other properties. I earned more money than any other salesperson in our office; more money than I had made in six months in my previous job. All in just 30 days!

My success was attributable to three factors. I was oriented to both our office and to real estate in general; I was well-trained and motivated; and I was hungry. I had heard about all of the money that could be made in real estate, and no one had bothered to tell me there would be obstacles, so there weren't any.

Chapter Three discusses the first of these factors: an effective orientation program. Making your new salespeople confident and professionally competent is an important first step in their (and your) selling success. It is the difference between John and a $2,000 a month or more producer, right from the very first month.

3-2. Eight Vital Areas that Should Be Included in Your Orientation Program

To be effective, your orientation program must familiarize the new agent with all aspects of your office, those people with whom he will be doing business, and his own capabilities and goals. The final result? In a brief period of time, you have made the new salesperson confident in his or her surroundings and part of a productive team.

Take nothing for granted, including where the rest rooms are, or where the agent should park. The most routine, obvious duties will never even occur to someone new in real estate. The most difficult part of designing an orientation program is putting yourself back in the place of a rookie and determining what questions you had when you started. Below is a list of eight vital areas your successful orientation must address. Each of these is important in developing the atmosphere and attitude required in a successful real estate office:

1. Handbook on office policy
2. Introduction to your present staff
3. Familiarization with your forms
4. Introduction to lenders, attorneys and closing agents
5. Personal survey of inventory
6. Placement with experienced agent
7. Review of past closings, expired listings and pending files
8. Goal-setting session

Now let's address these eight areas and how you can develop your own comprehensive orientation program. Your program, of course, should be complete, but it shouldn't become bogged down with more material than your new agents can comprehend within the participatory time period. Remember, this is not a training program. It is an introduction to the real estate profession in general and your office in particular. Limit your topics to these areas.

Present and oversee your orientation program personally. Do not leave this task to one of your salespeople or to your secretary. You will be presenting your new agent with the first look at his or her new profession and/or office. You want the agent to be impressed with your office and motivated by the opportunities a new career presents. Not only is this first step important enough for you to involve your own time, but you will also establish a closer relationship with your new salesperson.

3-3. Compiling a Handbook on Office Policy

One of the first differences I notice between professional, successful offices and mediocre offices is the presence of a well-thought-out, clearly defined office policy. Nothing does as much towards establishing a dynamic, professional atmosphere as guidelines concerning how you expect your associates to conduct their business.

As with anything, however, an office policy handbook can go overboard. It shouldn't serve as a tool to stifle creativity or aggressiveness. Often, I find policies that are negative rather than positive, and that are slanted totally toward the office. These handbooks serve as a deterrent to selling rather than as a motivator. As with any type of selling, your handbook should emphasize positive aspects, rather than communicate negative thoughts. Care should also be taken to ensure that your policy handbook does not infringe on the "Independent Contractor" status that you want to maintain with your salespeople.

An Example:

Sandifar-Misner Associates
Office Policy Handbook

From time to time questions will arise concerning the procedures and policies of this office. In an effort to familiarize you with the day-to-day operation of Sandifar-Misner Associates and provide you with guidelines for your relationship with your fellow salespeople, you are given guidelines that will help you overcome problems or answer questions.

You are an independent business person associated with Sandifar-Misner Associates, not an employee. As such, how you conduct your business is your personal choice. Since we want our association to be a positive and productive one, and one of which we can both be proud, however, we have listed a few guidelines that you are expected to abide by. Welcome to our Team of Professionals!

GENERAL GUIDELINES

1. *Sales Meetings*—A sales meeting for all associates is held each Tuesday morning at 9:00 a.m. Since information pertinent to your business is communicated during these meetings, your attendance is important to your success. If, for any reason, you are unable to attend any meeting, notify your sales manager in advance.
2. *Tour of Homes*—Each Thursday morning, beginning at 9:00 a.m., our entire staff inspects new listings taken dur-

ing the past week. Before you can talk about a property or sell it, you must be familiar with its features. Your attendance each week is imperative to your success.

3. *Floor Duty*—As an associate of Sandifar-Misner Associates, you will be provided floor duty time on a rotating basis. Each salesperson is given three (3) hours of floor duty, three (3) times weekly. Check the floor duty roster at the beginning of each month for your schedule. If for any reason you need to change any of your floor duty time, it is your responsibility to work out an equitable arrangement with another associate.

4. *Desk Space*—You will be provided a private desk. So that we may also present a professional appearance to the public, please keep your desk neat and uncluttered. Conference rooms are also available as needed for your meetings with clients, for research, etc.

5. *Advertising/Materials*—So that we can project a recognizable and positive image, it is important that all of our advertising conforms to previously developed formats.

    A. *Business Cards*—While your business cards are your responsibility, they should be consistent with those of your fellow associates. You will be provided a cut of our logo and company name to be printed on your business card.

    B. *Letters*—We encourage you to use letters as a means of prospecting and canvassing. There will also be specific instances when professional letters are needed. To help you, we have maintained a file of proven, time-tested letters. Each provides you a format for different types of mailings. Your sales manager will be happy to assist you with your letter.

    C. *Institutional Advertising*—Many of our salespeople use institutional advertising to keep their names before the public. When using institutional advertising, we ask that you use our logo and name as designed for your business cards and that you use sound judgment in the type of advertising you do. Please check with your sales manager before utilizing this type of advertising.

    D. *Ad Copy/Open Houses*—Since you (as listing agent) know more about a new listing than anyone else, turn in an ad copy with your new listing. While our advertising department will write the daily ads, you will be responsible for writing copy for open houses.

6. *Signs*—Sandifar-Misner Associates will provide signs for each listing and an open house sign for each agent. You are responsible for placing a "For Sale" sign on your listing during the tour of homes, or before, if needed. The "For Sale" sign is the responsibility of the listing agent. Each time you put a sign on the property, record it in the "Sign Book." You are also responsible for picking up the sign when the property is sold or the listing expires. Once you have retrieved the sign, record it in the "Sign Book," also.

   If you are the selling agent, you are responsible for placing a "Sold" sign on the property and picking up the "Sold" sign after a reasonable period of time. These should also be recorded in the "Sign Book."

7. *Expenses*—Only the expenses for the items below are paid for by Sandifar-Misner Associates. All others are the responsibility of the agent.

   A. Offer to purchase contracts
   B. Listing agreements
   C. Forms required by office
   D. Office-Sponsored handouts
   E. Office-Sponsored advertising
   F. Telephone expenses
   G. Listing presentations
   H. "For Sale," "Sold," and "Open House" signs (Inserts are the responsibility of the salesperson.)
   I. Listing book and copies of listings
   J. Multiple list fees for new listings
   K. All office expenses for utilities, cleaning, secretarial staff, etc.

   Any expenses incurred due to the processing of a transaction, such as legal expenses, abstract fees, appraisal fees, etc., will be deducted from the commission and shared proportionately by the selling agent, the listing agent, and Sandifar-Misner Associates. Other offices involved in the transaction will not be expected to share in these expenses unless they have a legal obligation to do so.

8. *Secretarial Staff*—Our secretaries are provided to assist you in maintaining a successful business. Please remember, however, that they must also serve your fellow associates, so be considerate of your demands on their time.

9. *Telephone Procedures*—The telephone is one of your most valuable tools. Use it! So that we may be able to maintain

our budget, please record your long distance phone calls on the phone log and turn it in to your sales manager weekly.

10. *Keys*—When you receive a key for a new listing, place a tag on it and put it in the appropriate location on the key board. The key board also has tags with your name on it. When you check out a key, please place your name tag on the empty key hook. Remember, if your fellow sales associates can't get into a property, they can't sell it. Please return each key immediately after showing the property. If another office picks up the key, place the salesperson's business card on the empty hook.

11. *Offers to Purchase*—Immediately upon receiving an offer to purchase on a property, record the offer in the "Offer Book." Once the offer has been accepted or rejected, record the price and financing method in the "Offer Book."

    All offers must be given to the listing agent immediately, along with any information he may need. If more than one offer is received, each should be presented simultaneously, and without prejudice.

    Before presenting an offer, the listing agent should check the "Offer Book" to ensure that no other offers have come in prior to the presentation.

12. *Pending Files*—Each transaction must have an up-to-date pending file until closing. This file should be maintained by the selling agent.

13. *Changes Book*—To ensure timely communication of all factors affecting each property, a "Change Book" will be maintained. Information contained includes price changes, listing extensions and expirations, changes on terms, any new information on listings, occupancy changes, new phone numbers for listings, etc.

    As listing agent, any changes on your listings should be recorded immediately. All agents should check the "Change Book" on a daily basis to remain informed.

14. *Message Box*—Each salesperson is assigned a message box. It also has the hands of a clock on it, indicating the time of your anticipated return. You should check in regularly to get your messages. Always set your clock, so the secretaries will know when to expect your return.

    Since phone calls mean commissions, it is important that our secretaries know where to reach you. Keep them informed.

15. *Client Control*—To ensure harmony and prevent disputes, the following policy on client control will be adhered to by all associates:

    A. If a call or walk-in prospect asks for a specific salesperson, that prospect belongs to him. Otherwise, the prospect should be followed up by the floor duty salesperson.

    B. If, for some reason, the salesperson asked for is not available and action must be taken immediately, the selling commission will be split 50-50 between the actual selling agent and the agent asked for.

    C If you are going to be on vacation, or cannot handle a client for some reason, refer your clients to a fellow agent. Inform the secretaries and your sales manager of any such arrangements, so they will know where to direct your calls. A 50-50 split is recommended in such cases, but the actual agreement should be worked out between you and the agent with whom you are working.

    D. Referrals of prospects entitle the referring agent to 10 percent of the commission. Any other arrangements should be agreed upon in advance.

    E. Any disputes concerning client control should be presented to your sales manager. After each side has been heard and the sales manager has made an investigation, he will issue a decision for settling the dispute.

    F. We are a professional team. Our relationship with each other is important to the success of everyone. One commission is not worth the hard feelings that result from unethical practice, particularly with regard to clients. The soliciting of another agent's client or prospect will not be tolerated.

16. *Commissions*—Commission rates are as follows:

No commission may be reduced without the approval of your sales manager.

$750 minimum commission	
Residential Property	6%
New Homes and Farms	5%

<table>
<tr><td>Bare Land</td><td>10%</td></tr>
<tr><td>Commercial Property</td><td>7%</td></tr>
</table>

Note: Sandifar-Misner Associates will waive (or refund) its portion of any commission on a home purchased or sold by one of our associates if it is their own personal residence.

17. *Files*—Files are maintained on closed or pending transactions, and expired listings. We recommend you use these files as a source of information, leads, and comparison for appraisals.

18. *Servicing Listings*—Servicing the listing is the responsibility of the listing agent. This includes canvassing the immediate area with "For Sale" cards, communicating with the seller, and handling any problems that may occur.

19. *Forms*—To assist you in becoming and remaining a top producer, Sandifar-Misner Associates provides you with several forms. Their uses are discussed below:

    A. *Property Showing Report*—Showing Agent: Complete the report and give it to the listing agent. Listing Agent: Discuss the report with the seller and maintain it in property file.

    B. *Telephone Inquiry Report*—A proven format for taking floor duty calls.

    C. *Daily Worksheet Report*—Complete one daily and review it with the sales manager during your personal monthly meeting.

    D. *Goal/Income Report*—Complete your goal form after each goal-setting session with your sales manager. Each month, complete the income section and review it with the sales manager during your personal monthly meeting.

    E. *Progress Report*—To be completed on each transaction as the closing progresses.

    F. *Prospect Data Card*—Maintain these for leads and as a record of contacts.

    G. *Competitive Market Analysis*—To be completed for each listing presentation.

    H. *Housing Requirement Analysis*—To be completed during initial meeting with each prospective buyer.

20. *Dress*—As a member of the Sandifar-Misner Associates team, your projected image is important to all of us. Male associates should wear suits and ties. Female associates should dress in a professional manner.

21. *Sales Manager*—Your sales manager has but one goal: to support and to serve you in a way that will enable you to be a top producer. He does not compete with you, or control you. Please call upon him at any time for any help you might need or to answer any questions you may have.

WELCOME ABOARD!

Prepare your handbook so that it fits into a loose-leaf binder. As your office grows or as changes become necessary, you can then add, delete, or change any part of it easily. Order several binders with your company name on the exterior and put your new agent's name on the cover with a plastic imprinted tape.

3-4. Introducing New Agents to Your Present Staff

While it has probably been a few years since you experienced this uncomfortable moment, stop to remember when you walked into your new office, and another salesperson said, "Can I help you?" It was a blow to your ego, as well as embarrassing to respond, "Oh, well no, actually, I work here."

Not only does common courtesy dictate that you personally introduce your new agent to his fellow associates, but it is also important if you are to make him or her feel comfortable in the new surroundings. The easiest way to handle this duty is to introduce your rookie at a sales meeting as soon as a decision has been made. He or she will have an opportunity to become acquainted with everyone, as well as immediately begin to feel like part of the team by listening to the presentation.

3-5. Familiarizing New Agents with Your Forms

As I've stated before in previous books, and will reiterate later in this one, that the first thing I notice about unproductive sales-people is that they don't know what they have done, or are presently doing, or will be doing in the future. Getting your sales-people started on using the right forms from the very first day, so they don't know any other way, is imperative to consistent successful selling. Although Chapter Nine discusses specifically what forms you should have and how to use them, here I will briefly discuss getting your new agents started using forms as a part of your orientation program.

These forms are designed with a very specific purpose in mind. They are not just used to generate paperwork. In fact, they are very simple to understand and complete, and they require very little of the agent's time. Your new associate should be given a supply of the following forms, instructions on how to complete and use them, and your explanation of the purpose of each.

A. Daily Worksheet Report
B. Goal Form (review it to prepare the rookie for your goal-setting session)
C Telephone Inquiry Report
D. Prospect Data Card
E. "House for Sale"
·F. "Introducing Your New Neighbor"
G. Prospect Showing Report
H. Listing Agreements
I. Offers to Purchase
J. Daily Schedule
K. Progress Report
L. Housing Requirement Analysis
M. Monthly Income Record

Briefly go through each form and have sample forms completed so your new agent can better visualize how to complete the form and how it will help him or her in business.

3-6. *Introducing New Agents to Lenders, Attorneys, and Closing Agents*

This part of your orientation program serves two purposes. When you personally introduce your newest agent to lending officers, your firm's attorneys, and to closing agents, you not only acquaint the rookie with people with whom he or she will need to work on each transaction, but also you will have made the road much smoother. For him to walk in and say, "Hello, I'm Mark Robinson with Sandifar-Misner Associates," assures him of a normal, courteous response. But if *you* say, "Dick, I'd like you to meet Mark Robinson. Mark is a new agent with Sandifar-Misner Associates, and *I know* you will give him as much help as you give me," this tells the other party, "He's one of ours. Take care of him."

You should also take the opportunity to inform your new agent of the positive and negative points of each of these individuals. Explain to him or her how to work with these people and how they can help lead to success.

3-7. Giving New Associates a Personal Survey of Your Inventory

Handing your new salesperson a copy of your listing book is not enough. Can you imagine an automobile salesman trying to sell a car from an ad, without ever having seen the car? Of course not. Neither can a real estate agent sell a house if he or she has never seen it.

Select three of four representative listings and accompany your new agent through them. Point out what he or she should look for and about what callers are likely to be inquisitive. Encourage the new agent to make his or her own notes on each property, so its image will stand out when he or she is called upon to discuss a particular property.

Once the new agent has a feel for inspecting property, have him or her make appointments to go through each listing. If the rookie has difficulty getting into a property, get the assistance of the listing agent. Not only is this procedure informative, but also it is very motivating. You have the agent thinking about how he or she would show each property, what features to highlight and in which area the tour would best be concluded. Each time the new agent inspects a choice listing, he or she will mentally consider to whom it might be sold. The rookie is itching to get turned loose with prospective buyers. These inspections will be more motivating than anything else you might tell the new agent at this point.

3-8. Placing Rookies with Experienced Agents

Careful! This decision could make a good salesperson or it could ensure failure. Stop and think about what your goal is here.

You want the new agent to gain field experience, using proven, successful techniques, so that he or she will know only the right things to do when starting out alone.

The point is, you may not want your top producer to be your trainer, or you may want it that way, depending upon how good his or her techniques are. If your star "cuts corners" or uses personal relationships with his or her prospects as an edge, this is *not* the person to train the new kid on the block. At this point, your concern is to teach proven techniques, not personalities. That comes later.

Your new salesperson should only need to be in the field with an experienced agent through one offer to purchase and one successful listing presentation. To continue this aspect of the educational process any longer is to deprive the new agent of full commissions and to drain his or her enthusiasm. The rookie will also begin to pick up the bad habits of the experienced agent if there is too much of an opportunity to see him or her work.

An equitable commission split is 50-50 if the client belongs to the new agent. I should add here that field experience should be gained by the new agent while working with his or her own prospects. Otherwise, the incentive and enthusiasm needed will not be present.

3-9. *Review of Past Closings, Expired Listings, and Pending Files*

The benefits your new salesperson will receive from the portion of your orientation program involving reviewing of past closings, expired listings and pending files are threefold:

1. They will become familiar with completed forms, transactions, and procedures;

2. They will gain enthusiasm and motivation from reviewing these files; and

3. They will pick up valuable leads from expired listings and past sales.

The key to your new associate's deriving these benefits rests with you. *How* they review your files will determine *what* they get from them. Keep in mind the three above goals you hope your agents will attain. Often, understudies have to be told what they will learn if they are expected to learn it. Tell them *what* these files will teach them and *how* they can use the files to generate income.

For instance, from reviewing the closing files, as well as the pending files, they will begin to get a feel for how to put a transaction together and how to use different financing methods. By reviewing the expired listings file, they can better understand how to complete a listing agreement and what information should be contained, as well as pick up leads for listing prospects. Past closings (three years or older) of agents no longer with your office will also provide your new associates with valuable leads.

3-10. *Planning a Goal-Setting Session*

You know the value of a well-defined, attainable goal. It's of special importance to new salespeople, however, since they most assuredly need the guidance and motivation it can provide. The people new to real estate sales (as well as many experienced agents) will neither know how to determine their goals, nor how to reach them, without your help. Your goal-planning session with them is an all-important step to their future success.

To ensure that you help them establish a successful goal, design your session as follows, discussing:

A. Income goal for the remainder of the year.

B. Break the goal down into a monthly income goal.

C. Average selling commission for your office.

D. Average listing commission for your office.

E. Number of monthly sales and sold listings needed to reach their goal.

F. Number of showings needed to make "x number" of sales.

G. Number of listings needed to have "x number" sold.

H. Number of listing presentations needed to list "x number."

I. Number of contacts needed to get "x number" of showings and appointments for listing presentations.

J. Number of hours per day necessary to spend on prospecting, canvassing, following up leads, etc.

After writing down the answers to these criteria, you and your new agents will know exactly what it takes for them to reach their income goal.

3-11. Instituting Your Sales-Generating Orientation Program

You now have an orientation program that makes your new associate comfortable, informed, motivated, and enthusiastic. You have taken the first, and the biggest, step towards turning a raw recruit into a million-dollar-a-year producer. To be successful, though, each step of this program must be incorporated into the indoctrination of every new associate, even if he or she has been selling real estate with another office. Implemented properly, it will shape his or her attitude into the same, self-assured, successful attitude maintained by the rest of your staff.

4

Developing a Successful Training Program

In today's real estate industry, training and training programs are in the forefront of every sales manager's concerns. Not only is the most up-to-date training available needed in order to get the most production possible out of your salespeople, your salespeople and prospective salespeople demand a comprehensive training program from their broker.

A national survey recently concluded that 70 percent of all brokers and sales managers said training and training tools were their single biggest problem. Likewise, when a salesperson is considering which office to join, over 80 percent list training as their number one priority in selecting an office. When asked why they had chosen to join a franchise, brokers listed the training programs available to them as second only to national recognition.

Even when the buying and selling public is decreasing due to high interest rates, economic instability, or inflated housing prices, the number of real estate salespeople in the market continues to increase. Today's new agents are made up differently than those of five or ten years ago. They are better educated, more professional and demand effective training programs to help them succeed in this very competitive business. Chapter Four reviews the training needs of real estate companies and some of the more successful programs available. We will also consider how you can compete with offices that offer full-time training directors and provide more training with less personal management than ever before.

4-1. *Ensuring Success with Proven Real Estate Selling Techniques*

Today's training programs have become much more sophisticated than earlier programs. In many cases, they have also become more expensive. The choice of programs available to you is extensive, and can easily cost you several thousand dollars. Still, these programs are much less expensive than hiring a full-time training director, or taking yourself away from other areas of your real estate business.

Sales managers buy training programs, or develop training programs for the same reason salespeople want to be trained: to increase the agent's ability to succeed, as rapidly and for as long as possible. Motivational programs alone will not meet this goal, nor will cassette tapes by themselves. A blend of seminars, audio/visual tapes, field exercises, and training tapes are necessary to develop the individual in an effective and lasting manner. Of course, if you attempt to utilize every program on the market, you will not only go broke, your program will fall short of your goal, because there will be no consistency to what you are trying to develop in your salespeople.

The question than becomes, "How can you ensure the success of your training program?"

First, select only those programs that teach proven, successful real estate selling techniques. Tapes that are strictly motivational or developed for a broad range of salespeople will not enable you to reach your goal of effectively training real estate salespeople. Their effect will be short-lived, and will not provide the agent with the techniques needed in different situations to be encountered in the field.

Second, review the material; then, in the field, try for yourself the techniques given. Do they really work? Are they techniques you feel comfortable using? Are they easily introduced into your style of presentation or your personality? If you, an experienced manager, cannot make the techniques work effectively, it is doubtful that your salespeople will enjoy success with them.

Third, does the material address every situation encountered by your agents in the field? Does the training provide role playing for your agents to listen to and watch, and to imagine themselves in the same situation? Salespeople learn in two ways: by watching the techniques being performed by someone else, and then by putting those techniques into their own presentation and practicing them.

Your last concern is the presentation itself. If it is not motivating enough to keep your salespeople interested, they will not retain the lessons provided. If you have to be present to administer the program, the program becomes too cumbersome to be effective, relying on your time schedule rather than that of the salespeople. If your program is too basic, your advanced salespeople will not profit from it, and it can only take your new salespeople to a certain point before it is no longer of any value to them.

4-2. *Fifteen Critical Areas Your Training Program Should Include*

Following is a checklist your training program should include to ensure that you have addressed every need of your agents. Some of these can be purchased with existing training programs, while others must be developed, by you, for inclusion with any purchased materials.

4-2A. *Technical Competence*

One of the restraints new salespeople, particularly females, put on themselves is the feeling that the buyer or seller knows more about structural soundness, mechanical systems, and design than the agent. Because of this, they are often reluctant to correct their prospect if he complains or worries about a certain feature of the home. Since one of the responsibilities of a real estate professional is to be able to recognize flaws and protect the buyer and seller, this aspect of your training program should be among the first administered to your agents. An excellent, complete, and comprehensive book is available to your agents concerning construction, design, and how to use these as selling tools. The book, entitled, *Real Estate Encyclopedia of Home Design, Construction and Architecture,* by Leonard Kleeman, published by Prentice-Hall, will make any agent feel like an expert. It should be a part of every real estate office library.

4-2B. *Time and Activity Management*

Real estate salespeople normally come from fields that do not require time and activity management since it has always been provided by superiors or else there was no need for it. Since time is the only restriction placed on the amount of money an agent can earn, it becomes his most precious asset, as well as his most dreaded enemy. Your program should include instruction on the most efficent and productive uses of time. What activities are the most profitable and what times are best for which activities? Show your agents how to work smarter, not harder and longer. If six good, productive hours a day, five days a week, were devoted to selling real estate, each of your agents would earn in excess of $30,000 per year.

4-2C. Prospecting

Most agents do not put nearly as much time into prospecting as they should. Many of those that do devote a portion of each day to this activity do not make the most productive use of their efforts. Your program should not only tell them how to prospect, but also where to prospect. They should be taught to utilize direct mail campaigns, high turnover areas, the telephone, and those people they know who are most likely to be aware of buyers and sellers.

4-2D. Canvassing

Agents are more likely to look favorably on canvassing if you can provide them with techniques that produce results and do not make them feel like they are just knocking on the door to ask for a listing. One of the most important canvassing activities is the development and maintenance of a farm system. If you provide your agents with a high turnover territory, a system for staying in touch with the residents, a reason to be in the neighborhood, and a technique for getting the door open, they will not only be productive, they will also enjoy their canvassing activity.

4-2E. Recognizing and Following Up on Leads

You and I know that leads to buyers and sellers are everywhere. You must provide enough training in this area to teach your agents to not only recognize potential leads, but also with a system by which to follow up on those leads.

4-2F. Making Appointments

It is not enough to simply train your agents how to give a listing presentation or how to show a property. Their problem is much deeper than that. Many feel comfortable once they are in the selling process, but do not feel comfortable getting to that point. They don't know how to make the appointment or suggest a meeting. Even if they do ask for an appointment, they do not set up their prospects to ensure that the salesperson is in control. Don't overlook this point when developing your training program.

4-2G. *Listing Presentations*

Each salesperson should have a professional listing presentation. Even if he or she doesn't use it in the field, by putting together a presentation and watching professionals use one, he or she will be more competent and better prepared with sellers in their livingrooms. Your training on preparing and using a listing presentation should include dialog from the moment the agent walks in the door until he or she walks out. Don't just show the agent how to use the presentation and leave him or her there, not knowing how to ask for the listing or the price, or to educate the sellers on the selling process their home will go through.

4-2H. *Showing Techniques*

From the time your agent meets the client until he or she asks for the offer-to-purchase, he or she is conditioning the buyer to make a buying decision. Your program should include each step in this process. As with all aspects of your training procedure, your agents should be exposed to video role playing, workbooks, and then actual field and role-playing experiences.

4-2I. *Closing Techniques*

Thoroughly review each closing technique with your salespeople. Encourage them to practice each over and over, until they become a very natural part of their vocabulary.

4-2J. *Overcoming Objections*

There is no reason for your agents not to know well in advance every objection the buyer or seller could possibly offer. Their responses should be automatic, logical, and timely. Give them the proper response and have them re-hearse each until they feel comfortable.

4-2K. *Creative Financing*

Even if your agents don't handle their own financing, they should be aware of every avenue, of the requirements for each, and how to put together several methods of financing to close a transaction. If they don't understand creative financing, they will never get the client into the financing department in the first place.

4-2L. *Closing Procedures*

Make sure your agents understand their responsibilities in each step of the closing process. Show them how to complete the proper forms, when and where to order the legal work, how to order insurance, and to follow-up after the closing.

4-2M. *Advertising*

Almost every office requires its agents to either write their own ads or to turn in the first ad copy with their listing, yet few provide the agent with any formal training of what an ad should contain, how it should be written, and the response they want it to generate. You should also discuss the effects and various methods of institutional advertising.

4-2N. *Office Policy*

As discussed in Chapter Eight, office policy is an important part of your effort to develop the proper attitude and atmosphere within your office. Use your training program as the catalyst for this all-important aspect of the salesperson's responsibility.

4-2O. *Presenting Offers*

Your training tapes should once again include role playing of this final step in the negotiating process. After reviewing films and tapes, and completing workbook studies, your agent should practice on you or other agents. Again, there is no reason for the agent to be surprised by the objections or attitudes of the seller. Your program should discuss how to prepare for the presentation, how to make the appointment, how to present the offer, how to overcome objections, how to close, and how to get a counter-offer.

4-3. *Using Successful Training Tools and Techniques*

Poorly developed or unprofessional training tools and techniques cause more harm than good. If you develop bad habits in your salespeople, or if they are not convinced of the technique being taught them, the result will be worse than if they had no training at all. Your agents will eat up territory, get discouraged because of failure, and become dissatisfied with your program.

In short, don't train for the sake of training. Don't buy a program because it is cheap. Don't institute your own training unless it is based on professionally prepared programs. The best salesperson in the world is seldom the best teacher. You may know how to succeed at selling, but do you have the ability to communicate your knowledge and technique to your salespeople? After all, your purpose is to enable your agents to develop their abilities to the greatest extent possible, not to merely do your duty by instituting a training program.

A shortcoming of many purchased training programs is that they do not provide the sales manager with the tools necessary to sponsor the training. Any program you purchase should also have a trainer's guide that relieves you of the responsibility of preparing the text or organizing the teaching. You should be able to actually read, word for word, from the guide, the instructions and ideas you want to present to your agents. The program should be designed in a manner that allows any agent to take the training, or any part of it, on his own, without the constant attention of the sales manager.

By implementing successful training tools and techniques that are designed to meet the needs of your agents and their particular problems, you can expect to increase each salesperson's income by twenty-five to fifty percent. Considering the potential benefit to you and your salespeople, it is in your best interest to take the time and effort to investigate the program you select prior to purchase, and not be afraid to spend a few thousand dollars for the right one(s).

4-4. Taking Advantage of the Most Up-to-Date Training Techniques

As with any industry, the field of training has progressed tremendously over the past few years. New techniques, material, and approaches to training have developed to the point that almost any office can afford them, and even advanced salespeople can increase their income by taking the training offered. Offices that have not updated their training programs in the past two or three years are not enjoying the benefits offered by today's technology. They are also not keeping up with their competition. While you can't buy every program offered you, take the time to review the material you receive so that you will be aware of the advances being made and how you can incorporate them into your program.

Following is a list of those programs that have proven to be successful for today's real estate agent:

Performance Plus Learning System—This training program, developed for and available only to Red Carpet brokers, is a two-track system that enables your agents to train at different times and different levels. A high quality audio/video program with workbooks, it is the only two-track system being offered today. Your advanced agents use the same video tapes but a different workbook, so a new agent can be trained at the same time as an advanced agent, without one of them being bored or having the material used so far over his head that it's useless. The program incorporates role playing with actual field experience and requires only ten to fifteen minutes of the sales manager's time each day.

Passport to Potential—Danny Cox, one of the premier teachers and motivators of real estate salespeople today, has produced a long playing album concentrating on what it takes to be successful, both as a salesperson, and as a human. A proven, successful real estate agent and sales manager himself, Danny offers a program to salespeople that has been proven in the field.

Manager's Guide to Higher Productivity—Also by Danny Cox, this cassette series offers eight hours of training of the real estate sales manager, utilizing the same techniques that enabled him to put together an astonishing record of increased production and reduced turnover in his offices. In one year alone, his office took 1,737 listings, selling 1,570 of them, with total sales of $166,100,000. The program includes advice on building a winning team, reducing turnover, interviewing and recruiting, goal setting, personal growth as a manager, getting new people started on the right foot, how to motivate, how to put together sales meetings that everyone wants to attend, successful cold group telephone canvassing, leadership, and many other areas of managing a real estate office, including one of the most creative and successful advertising concepts on the market today.

Both of Danny Cox's programs are available from:

> Danny Cox Seminars
> 1111 Town and Country Rd.
> Suite 40
> Orange, CA 92668

Tom Hopkin's Champions Unlimited—Fastart™ Video Training Program—One of the best selling training programs in the country, *FASTART™* includes 30 Video Cassettes, Workbooks, flashcards, Instructor's Manual, recruiting brochures, and additional motivational items. The Tom Hopkins *FASTART™* Video System offers you the benefits of a continuous, in-house training program, and is an excellent recruiting tool.

How to Master the Art of Listing Real Estate/How to Master the Art of Selling Real Estate—Both of these programs feature Tom Hopkins, and provide your salespeople with fast, proven lessons of how to succeed at these two all-important aspects of real estate selling. All three of these programs are available through:

> Tom Hopkins Champions Unlimited
> 7531 East 2nd St.
> Scottsdale, AZ 85251
> 1-800-528-0446, Ext. 312

Jerry Park's Master Plan for Increased Success in Real Estate—Jerry Parks is owner of Regal Realtors in Dallas, Texas. Besides a successful career as a broker and real estate salesman, Jerry has written two books on selling real estate and operates the largest real estate school in the state of Texas. His tape cassette series is an excellent training guide for real estate agents.

Jerry Parks
2725 Valley View Lane
Dallas, TX 75234

4-5. *How Other Real Estate Offices Have Designed and Implemented Training Programs that Create Successful Salespeople*

Fairfax Realty is a very successful real estate office. By today's standards they would be considered small, employing only eleven salespeople. However, they have the largest sales volume of any agency in their community, even though many of the other real estate firms are two or three times as large.

Their salespeople earn more than any other agents in town, with their lowest producer exceeding the top producer in most offices. The make-up of Fairfax's staff is interesting, in that:

A. This is the only office any of them have ever been associated with.

B. Their experience in real estate runs from one to ten years.

C. Their ages range from 22 to 54 years old.

D. They have varied backgrounds, but all are people-oriented. Their former professions included: teaching, selling building supplies, selling in retail stores, and personnel administering; the group also included two store owners, a secretary, a banker, a businesswoman, and a tire salesman.

As you can see, experience, background, and age alone cannot account for their unusual success. They all do have one thing in common, however: the company's training program. Believing in quality and the individual success of the salesperson, rather than in large numbers, Fairfax has developed a personal, one-on-one training program. Their sales manager worked with each agent when he or she joined the company. Besides providing training in selling, listing, prospecting, etc., the sales manager worked with each individual to strengthen his or her weaknesses and to help develop successful selling techniques that matched each one's personality. The Fairfax program consists of the following parts:

1. An introduction to the use and purpose of the company's forms.

2. Tapes and articles on showing, listing, canvassing, presenting the offer, and overcoming objections.

3. Each aspect of the program is given a dry run, using the sales manager in a vacant home, or a fellow agent at a sales meeting as a client.

4. The new agent is put into the field with the agent who is the best teacher, not necessarily the best salesperson.

5. Besides the initial training, each sales meeting involves the agents themselves in training sessions. Role playing is used each week to develop techniques for listing presentations, canvassing, presenting offers, taking floor duty calls, etc. This allows all of the agents to benefit from seeing how their associates perform a particular function well, or it can help the agent who does not do something well by reviewing his or her performance.

6. As the sales manager discovers new material, books or articles that will improve the agents' ability to succeed at selling, he or she purchases a copy for every agent and makes it required reading.

This program is not expensive or complicated. It does take the personal attention and devotion of many hours on the part of the sales manager.

Taft Realty, on the other hand, must take an entirely different approach to training, since it employs over 100 salespeople in five offices. The sales managers do not have the time to devote to their agents for one-on-one training. Instead, they depend on two other methods for providing their agents with the training they need. First, they have general, regularly scheduled group training sessions, and second, they initially place new agents with experienced agents.

A. The general group sessions are held weekly for the new agents at a central location. A training director instructs recruits on each aspect of selling real estate, shows training films, and provides the new agents with their own workbooks from which they are expected to practice the techniques they are taught each week. Part of each session is allotted to role playing, by the participants, of the subject covered during the previous week. After an agent has completed the six-week training course, he or she joins the other agents in monthly training sessions designed to sharpen their skills and reinforce proven selling techniques.

B. For the first six weeks, the new agent is also assigned to an experienced agent in the field. The new agent develops prospects and then is joined for all appointments by the other agent. The senior agent is expected to report on the progress of the rookie, as well as train him or her.

Reading and tapes are relied on heavily in Taft's program, since the agent must spend many more hours in training than management can give him or her personally.

Gunther Real Estate, Inc. falls between the other two offices, employing 36 salespeople with one office location and a part-time branch office. Not large enough to offer a full-time training director, but too large to devote themselves to one-on-one training, Gunther Real Estate relies on a pre-programmed training system that each salesperson can progress through at his/her own pace.

After three initial two-hour sessions with the sales manager, that cover those areas not included in the formal training program, the agent is expected to spend two hours per day viewing video cassette tapes. He or she is then required to practice the techniques given, and work in the field that afternoon on those particular selling techniques that were learned during the morning session. Five minutes are spent with the sales manager the following morning, reporting on the outcome of the rookie's use of the technique in the field.

Gunther only assigns experienced agents with the recruits for their first listing and sale, to ensure a smooth transaction and take pressure off of the new agents. After that, the new agents are on their own, unless they request help from the sales manager, or if the sales manager finds a problem during their personal sales meetings.

On-going training for all salespeople is provided during the sales meeting each week, with two special evening sessions conducted during the year.

4-6. Judging the Success of Your Training Program

How many students have failed a subject, not because of their inability to learn, but rather because of the teacher's inability to teach? Coming from a family of educators, I have always known that the success of a teaching method, aid, or teacher shows up in the success of the student. If the student doesn't grasp the subject, and isn't more knowledgeable because of it, he hasn't failed; the system or the teacher failed.

The same holds true for your training program. If your agents are not more enthusiastic and more successful after they have participated in your training program, it isn't because they aren't trainable or aren't good—it's because the program isn't good. You must be able to provide training that is effective, and be able to judge that effectiveness.

You can be alert to the success of the training you provide your salespeople in the following ways:

A. Feedback—Are the agents excited? Do they use the techniques you are teaching? Are their comments favorable or nonexistent?

B. Increased Activity—Are your agents making more calls? Having more showings? Arranging more appointments? Are they working more in the areas you have been discussing?

C. Commissions—The bottom line is "Are they making higher earnings than ever before?"

If the answer is *no,* look toward your program, not your agents. It is your responsibility to provide the agent with successful techniques. Not successful techniques for you, or for me—but successful for your agents. Change your program until you hit upon the tools and techniques that make your salespeople successful. Then, and only then, will your training program be successful.

5

Teaching Proven And Effective Listing Techniques To Double Your Listing Inventory

"The office that controls the listings controls the market. Listings are your inventory, and without them you have nothing to sell."

How many times have you given this speech to your salespeople? Every sales manager, as well as every agent, knows these statements to be true. Yet, getting your agents to spend a considerable amount of their time on listings is practically impossible. In Chapter Five, we will take an in-depth look at why agents don't spend more time actively working listings, how you can overcome this problem, and how your agents can be more effective with their listing presentations and in uncovering potential listings. We'll also discuss how you can encourage your agents to reap all of the benefits and commission checks that listings provide them.

5-1. Understanding Your Agent's Inability to List

Seldom will your agent lose a listing due to competition. Surveys show that 78 percent of all homeowners who list their property do so with the first agent who contacts them. More important than technique then, or office image, is the agent's success at being the first real estate salesperson to make a contact with a potential seller. Realizing this fact, a sales manager has to ask why his or her agents aren't getting to the homeowners first. Before you can teach effective techniques, or succeed with your listing materials, you must get your salespeople to talk to sellers and ask for the listing.

Salespeople's inability to list is a restriction that they place on themselves. Until they have discovered the true benefits of listing success, they will not work listings because of the negative aspects they foresee. You will have to help the agents overcome the following prejudices before you can help them succeed with techniques, presentations, or marketing material.

5-1A. *Someone Has Already Been There*

Real Estate salespeople are hesitatnt to contact an owner when they find a lead that is available to all salespeople, because they believe several other agents have already made a contact and the seller has either already made a decision or has prepared his or her defenses in such a way that the agent will not be able to convince him or her to list the home with them. If this were true, the odds are that the property would already be listed, so the probability is that no one else has contacted the owner. However, even if they have, what is the cost of talking to the owner? A negative response is only a negative response. At worst, the owner says no. Big deal! But the owner can never say yes if the agent doesn't ask.

5-1B. *Listings Become a Headache*

There is a responsibility that goes with listing a property that many agents don't want to assume. If the property is overpriced or has a deficiency, the agent must relate this information to the owner. If the property is shown, the agent must explain to the seller why the buyers didn't make an offer. If the home isn't shown, the agent must explain why. Discussions with the owners become a hassle and the listing agent begins avoiding the sellers, rather than face them with reality.

The agent feels he or she hasn't lived up to the promises made during the listing presentation and is afraid to face the sellers. This mental game, or self-harrassment the agent puts him- or herself through, need never take place, if the agent adopts the proper attitude, and communicates as necessary with the sellers. A few rules for servicing the listing will enable your agents to rid themselves of problems with sellers forever.

1. It is not *your* problem, it is *theirs.* You are going to help the sellers solve their problem, not remove from them the burden of it. I make my clients aware of any problems with the listing.

2. Communicate with the seller regularly. Every time the property is shown, or, on a weekly basis if it is not shown, call or stop by and see the owners. Let them know what you are doing for them.

3. Tell them the bad news. The sellers did not just select you as the agent that should receive a listing commission. They hired you because you are the expert in real estate and they believed you could help them with their goal better than any other agent. If something needs to be repaired, if the price is too high, if terms are needed, or if buyers or agents make negative comments, inform your sellers. Tell them what they need to do to sell their home.

4. Work for them. Write ads that will generate responses. Hold open houses. Canvass the neighborhood. Contact other real estate agents. Communicate changes to office associates. If you honestly feel you are earning the opportunity the sellers gave you, you will not be ashamed to face them, even when the home is slow in moving.

5-1C. *The Reward Is too Far Down the Line*

How many of your agents tell you they are selling agents and not listing agents? What they are really saying is that they can immediately reap the rewards of an offer to purchase, but they might have to wait two, three, or four months to receive a listing commission for the effort they put forth today. For years, we sales managers and brokers encouraged this attitude by giving a larger portion of the commission to the selling agent than we did to the listing agent. Now, when we finally woke up and realized the error in our thinking, we suddenly expect our agents, whom we have spent years rewarding for selling rather than listing, to shed their beliefs over night and realign with our new philosophy.

It is not enough to merely change the commission schedule or begin preaching listings. You must also reshape the thinking of your salespeople. Show them that, while the rewards may be slower in coming, they are far greater and easier to attain than those realized from selling a home.

Once your agents have been convinced their concerns about listings, even though they may not be voiced, are simply restrictions they are placing on themselves, and that every other agent has the same concerns, you can begin teaching them how to improve their efficiency, recognize leads, and benefit from their listing inventory. But before you ever place them in a classroom, you must prepare them mentally for listing success by removing the doubts from their minds that are surely present.

5-2. Ten Time-Tested Avenues Your Agents Should Be Taking to Secure Listings

Be as creative as you want; there are still only so many sources for listing leads, and they have all been discovered. The secret is not in finding new sources, but rather in becoming attuned to these sources already available to you. We all see these sources, but only a few of us recognize them. Following is a list of ten sources your agents should be constantly searching for, and be able to recognize them when they see them.

5-2A. For Sale by Owner

The most obvious lead to a potential listing is the "For Sale By Owner." The possibility that an owner can secure a buyer, a fair price, and financing is extremely slim. Over 80 percent of all For Sale By Owners eventually list their property with a professional real estate agent. Not only is this market ripe, it is also one we must all actively work to convert because our biggest competitor is not another real estate office, but rather For Sale By Owners. This is not because of their volume, but because of the fact that, if they were successful, we would be out of business.

Remember, FSBO's normally list with those offices that contact them first. To insure that your agents are first in line and stay in contact with the sellers until a listing agreement is signed, implement the following program, including

1. A personal contact to determine price, owner's name, and reason for selling, and to offer to help if they secure a buyer.

2. A mailing campaign containing three pieces that are of interest to the For Sale By Owner. The first might be a letter reminding them of your desire to help, along with an insert that describes various methods of financing. Next, send a letter asking about their progress and include a blank offer, with the suggestion that they have something drawn up similar to it to protect themselves when they secure a buyer. The third letter would include a copy of your open house ads that they might want to use as a guide in advertising their home, along with a mention of what they can expect to pay for such an ad. Of course, in each letter, you close with the offer that should they need your help or if they decide to list their property, you would like to have an opportunity to explain to them what you and your company can do for them.

3. Ask for the appointment. There are a variety of reasons you can use get the owners to sit down and talk with you. You can offer to give them advice on what they might do to make their home more attractive to the buying public; you can offer to assist them when they secure a buyer by helping with the financing, in return for their providing you with leads of those buyers who made inquiries but weren't interested in their home; or offer to give them your presentation so that, when and if they decide to list their home, they will be aware of what services you have to offer.

This three-step approach to listing FSBO has enabled me to secure over 90 percent of the FSBOs I contact. Other agents

I have trained enjoy similar success with it, and not surprisingly, no agent who uses it has less than an 80 percent success record.

5-2B. *Newspaper Leads*

The daily and weekly newspapers in your community provide as many or more leads than any other source available. By reading the paper with an eye for listing opportunities, you find dozens of happenings that indicate an owner is about to become a potential seller. While some of the reasons are not pleasant, you didn't create the problem and somebody will have to handle the sale of the property. Search out the following and follow up on them as listing leads:

1. Marriages	14. Retirements
2. Births	15. Property Transfers
3. Transfers	16. Bankruptcies
4. Divorces	17. Foreclosures
5. Promotions	18. Business Openings
6. Business Closings	19. Position Wanted Ads
7. Deaths	20. Help Wanted Ads
8. Crime Convictions	(Yard and House Care)
9. Auctions	21. For Sale By Owner
10. Garage Sales	22. Tax Liens, Suits, etc.
11. Rental Houses	23. Lay-Offs
12. Business Moves	24. Acquisitions of Business
13. Graduations	

Twenty-Four different types of leads are available every day, just by looking in your newspaper. Your agents should never complain of not having adequate leads on which to follow up.

5-2C. *Drive-Bys*

By taking a different route to the same destination each day, your agents can uncover excellent listing leads by simply keeping their eyes open. Certain signs indicate a need to sell a property. Your agents have a better than even chance to win these listings, because often the owners themselves do not even realize their need to sell. A suggestion from an agent can spur a tired or distressed owner into action. The following signs should cause your agents to stop and investigate further.

1. Neglected property—exterior, yard, etc.
2. Vacant property
3. Moving vans (A tenant could be moving)
4. Elderly people working in the yard
5. "For Sale By Owner" signs
6. Another office's sign at the side or rear of the house
7. House being repaired
8. Builder constructing a house
9. "For Lease" signs
10. Houses near other office's "Sold" sign
11. Vacant lots
12. Children (Big house with no children in the yard, or small house with several children in the yard)

On a recent tour of homes our office is listing, seven of the listings were from one of the categories listed above. Your agents just have to have their eyes open.

5-2D. Business Associates

Regular contacts and providing referrals in return will enable your agents to generate numerous leads from attorneys, bankers, barbers, doctors, shopkeepers, and others with whom they do business every day. Your agents shouldn't hesitate to suggest that, if they are provided referrals and leads by their sources, they will return the favor. Insurance agents, particularly those with a debit route, are excellent sources for trading referrals.

5-2E. Builders

Your agents can establish a profitable working arrangement with builders that can benefit both parties. Builders attract buyers who already own a home, have built-up equity, and are now ready for a move to a more expensive home. Most builders do not have a means of helping these buyers dispose of their property, so they will often lose the buyer. Your agents can solve the builder's problem and increase their earnings by putting the package together in exchange for the listing on the buyer's home.

5-2F. Canvassing

Whether your agents develop a farm system, cold canvass, or work a neighborhood where they have just sold a property, canvassing does pay off in listings. Many agents dislike canvassing because of not having a productive dialog to use when the owner opens the door. The following reasons for knocking on the door will get the owner talking and provide valuable leads for the agent:

1. "I just sold the home down the street and I wanted to tell you about your new neighbor. We had several other buyers for that home. Do you know of anyone else considering selling in this area?"

2. "I just put Mr. and Mrs. Davis's home down the street on the market. Do you have any friends or relatives interested in moving into this neighborhood? Have you considered selling?"

3. "I specialize in homes in this area. I wanted to take a few minutes to introduce myself and see if you had considered selling your home or buying a new one. If you have a real estate need, please give me a call."

4. "I have a client who is looking for a home in this area. Since we don't have a home in this neighborhood, I wanted to take a few minutes to stop and talk with you about selling your home."

Your agents can also canvass via the telephone or direct mail. While these two methods are not as effective on a call-per-call basis, they can generate an even larger response from owners because of the large number of contacts that can be made in a relatively short period of time.

5-2G. Prospecting

As long as I've been in the real estate business and as many loyal clients as I am fortunate to have had, few ever call me and say, "Hey, I've got a good lead for you." On the other hand, they never hesitate to provide me with any leads they may be aware of if I ask them. Many times they will not even be aware that they have knowledge of a lead, since they are not professional salespeople. I make my living from their referrals, they make nothing by giving them to me. It is my responsibility and my opportunity to call acquaintances and seek qualified leads from them.

When I first entered real estate, I didn't have a backlog of clients and I hadn't been taking floor duty to supply me with a list of potential buyers and sellers. My sole source of business was the people I knew. By contacting them, I was able to sell seven homes, take five listings and have two listings sell in my first month in real estate. I was not a super salesman. I was twenty-one years old and knew nothing about selling. I just made contacts. If your agents aren't selling, they aren't making contacts.

5-2H. Buyers

As obvious as it may be to you and me, it is amazing the number of agents who seem to forget that buyers are often sellers, too. Your agents should treat every potential buyer or caller as a listing prospect and not concentrate solely on selling them a new home.

5-2I. Expired Listings, Closed Sales

Expired listings can be the most productive and profitable listings for real estate agents if they know how to take advantage of the market. Whether the listing is an old, expired listing of your office or a recently expired listing of another office, your agent has two very important elements in his or her favor. First, the owner still has a need to sell, and secondly, the owner has been educated as to price, terms, or conditions of the property. The fact that the home didn't sell the first time is evidence to the seller that what the first listing agent told him is true, and he or she must now bow to the wisdom of the professional in order to move the home.

Sales closed either in your or another office, more than three years ago, are also good leads to potential sellers. Since statistics prove that the average homeowner moves every three to five years, your agents have all of the information they need on a potential listing and good reason to believe that the owner has a need or desire to sell.

5-2J. Courthouse Records

As an experiment, John Whalen, of Whalen Real Estate, hired a courthouse clerk to give him a list of all owners of more than one parcel of real estate in the county, along with their addresses. With his list in hand, he divided the names among his salespeople and sent them out to contact these multi-property owners.

In the first week alone, John's agents generated a total of 22 listings along with many associations that resulted in business for years to come.

Courthouse records are public information and provide your agents with many leads if they take the time to review them and hire a clerk to do the research for them.

5-3. Implementing a Successful Farm System

Experience and research prove that contact with the buying public is the surest way to receive their business. While the process may be boring, regular visits, calls, or letters to owners will result in a steady flow of business for any agent. To acquire listings, the most successful method of steady contact is the farm system. While the first run may not result in many listings, as more repeat contacts are made, more referrals, listings, and leads will result.

Agents who fail with farm systems do so for three reasons. They canvass in "choice" areas everybody wants into, rather than high turnover areas that have a history of sellers; they do not devote enough time, on a regular basis, to working their farm; or they give up too easily if the farm doesn't pay off immediately. If your agents are failing with their farm systems, the reason lies in one of these three areas. Investigate to determine which is at fault, and help them correct their method of working the farm system.

Besides watching for the above mistakes, there are other actions you can take to ensure a successful farm system for your agents. The material you provide them as "hand-outs" is very important, and becomes the format of the letters you provide them with to mail to property owners within their farm area. A few hours on your part, spent designing a letter and selecting handouts, can dramatically increase your agents' production. If you leave these areas to your salespeople, few will do either, and those who do will not have the expertise or material available to them that you have.

Remember the rules of implementing a successful farm system:

1. Assign your agents high turnover areas.
2. Keep a close watch on the time they spend canvassing.
3. Make them stay with it, even if they aren't successful at first.
4. Provide them with useful handouts and effective letter formats.

5-4. Putting Together an Effective and Powerful Visual Aid that Puts Professionalism into Your Agents' Listing Presentations

Professional listing presentations use visual aids to present your story in a logical order that will eliminate the sellers' objections, increase the impact of what your agent is saying, and make it easier for the agent to concentrate on the seller and his or her reactions. When used, these are very effective tools, but few agents actually utilize what they have available to them. Few are also creative or artistic enough to put together a professional looking visual aid presentation. Because of the mass purchasing power and means available to you as sales manager, you are in the best position to purchase or put together an effective, powerful presentation that can be implemented into each of your agents' listing programs.

Perhaps the easiest method of providing your agent with a professional visual aid is to purchase one. Tom Hopkins Champions Unlimited produces an excellent presentation that can easily be adapted to the personality, abilities, and accomplishments of your salespeople. Considering the price and the professional style, this avenue is the most efficient one available to you.

If you have a large sales staff, however, or simply desire to put together your own visual aids, the following guide will help you put together an equally professional presentation.

Page 1:

Introduce your office. Include a color photo of the exterior and highlight those aspects of your office that will have an impact on the seller, such as length of service, office hours, specialties, etc.

Page 2:

Introduce the sales staff. If possible, use a group photo, but individual photos will suffice. Under the photo print: "A total of _____ years of experience in the real estate market."

Page 3:

Introduce the individual agent. Each agent should have a picture of him- or herself standing behind a sold sign, or one from an announcement of "Salesman of the Month." The agent should list those areas of accomplishment important to sellers such as; Licensed since _____ , Graduate of _____ State Licensing Course, Designations held, Member of _____ Board of Realtors, etc.

Page 4:

Use testimonials. Each agent should have letters of reference to offer the owner. These handwritten testimonials should highlight the agent's attention, thoughtfulness, professionalism, success, and dedication to the seller.

Page 5:

Use this page to show the owner why your agents are professionals and why this fact is important to him or her as a seller. Stress the continuing education, experience with financing, dedication to ethics, etc.

Page 6:

Here is where you begin to show the owner why a professional is needed to represent him or her, and why your agents are the best professionals available. On this page, list the various methods of financing and prepare your agents to tell the owner just enough about financing, what's available, and how it will affect the sale of his or her home by confusing the potential seller, and make him or her realize how little he really knows about financing.

Page 7:

Highlight the difference between what the sellers can do for themselves, what any real estate firm can do for them, and what you can do for them in addition to their and other offices' efforts.

Page 8:

Take a copy of your most impressive advertisement and make a full one- or two-page spread to impress the owners with the type of advertising to expect their home to receive.

Page 9:

Present the prospect showing report. Include a copy of the form and an explanation that the owner will be notified each time the home is shown, along with a discussion of the buyer's comments.

Page 10:

Explain the telephone inquiry report. Let the seller know that you are prepared to handle the calls you will receive on his or her home, and how this will be beneficial.

Page 11:

One of the objections your agents will receive from sellers is that they want another office to handle their sale because of their size or sales record. On this page, you are going to overcome that objection before it is expressed, and also impress the seller with the amount of exposure his or her home will receive.

On this page, include a typed copy of a listing or a multilist copy. Print the words, "Village Real Estate provides all of the essential information on your home to cooperating brokers."

Point out to the sellers that every agent in the area will be invited to show their home, so they have the benefit of hundreds of agents working for them at the same time. And, they still will get the professional and personal service you have to offer.

Page 12:

Include an offer to purchase with their name and address typed on it. Across the center of the offer write, "Sold." Your agent should explain to the seller, "Mr. and Mrs. Amyx, this is our obligation to you; to bring you an acceptable offer in the shortest length of time."

Page 13:

Insert a blank listing agreement. ". . . and *this* is your

obligation to us. As soon as we complete this form, we can begin working for you."

Page 14:

Use a Competitive Market Analysis. This form should be prepared so the agent can take it out when he or she begins discussing price with the seller.

Additional pages can be added to promote other aspects of selling a home as your agents desire. The quality of the visual aid is of utmost importance. You should go to the expense of utilizing the expertise of a local printer or graphics design expert. Following is a list of material you will need to construct each presentation.

- Free Standing Binder
- Plastic (Clear) Folders
- Black Construction Paper (Background)
- Office Letterhead Stationery
- Several Thin White Strips of Paper (For Captions)
- Photos
- Ad Copy
- Testimonials
- Forms
- CMA

5-5. Teaching Your Agents to Handle the "How much is it worth?" Question

Sellers always have one question in the back (or front) of their minds. What will they receive for their home? If your agents answer this question too quickly or incorrectly, they will lose the seller before they get to first base.

While several techniques can be employed to overcome this problem, none works better than the Competitive Market Analysis available from the National Association of Realtors. By first reviewing what similar homes have sold for recently and what those homes that haven't sold are listed at, the agent can lead the seller to the obvious conclusion of what price his or her home should be offered for. Owners beliefs, emotions, and false assumptions cannot match up against the facts concerning what their property is worth, based on the sales price of similar homes.

Now it is not just the agent's opinion; the suggested price is a result of market research. If the price brings a strong negative reaction from the seller, your agent has not backed him- or herself into a corner. The agent can still take the listing at the owner's price, with the understanding that the analysis does not show the higher value, but that if anyone can get it for the owner, your agent can.

5-6. Successful Techniques for Overcoming the Seller's Objections

Sellers can only offer a limited number of objections to listing their home with your agent. An agent who fully understands the objections he or she may face, and is prepared to overcome them, will succeed at securing the listing contract. Review the following objections and counters with your agents until they can use them as a natural part of their vocabulary and without surprise when the objections are offered by the seller.

Before overcoming any objection, the agent should take care to ensure that it is truly an objection, and not merely a smoke screen. Force the seller to reaffirm the objection, explain it, and give him or her an opportunity to discard it without your help.

Objection:	Last week an Agent from Ajax Realty said he could get me $65,000 for my home.
Agent:	An agent from Ajax said he could get you $65,000?

Stop! Let the seller respond. No matter the objection, repeat it to the seller and wait for the reply. This gives the agent two advantages. First, with further explanation, the agent can become more aware of the thinking of the seller and how important this particular objection is to him or her. Second, the agent gives the seller the opportunity to talk him- or herself out of the objection.

Assuming the agent has repeated the objection to the seller and the objection must be overcome, the following counters are easy for the agent to use, are logical to the seller, and have proven to be successful techniques for securing the listing.

Objection: We want to think it over.

Reply: "This is an important decision, Mr. Abrams, and I can understand your desire to give it every consideration. What is it that you feel you need to think over?"

Seller: "Well, I just want to be sure we are doing the right thing at this time."

Reply: "Let's review your situation, Mr. Abrams. You and Mrs. Abrams would like to have a larger home, wouldn't you? After reviewing the creative financing available, we know that not only can you expect to get good terms, but we can also offer buyers excellent terms on your home, which puts it ahead of the competition, isn't that right? We also know that this advantage will not be present if the interest rates start coming down. Your home will actually become less valuable because all homes will be available at similar cost, isn't that true? Mr. Abrams, everything seems to indicate that now is the time to put your home on the market, doesn't it? By putting your home on the market this evening, we can get a jump on everyone else who will soon be putting their homes up for sale, and we can also start working on putting you and your family into the new home you want." (Hand him back the listing and your pen.) "Just okay this agreement on the bottom line, please."

Objection 2: We aren't ready to sell our home yet. We want to wait until school is out.

Reply: "I don't blame you for not wanting to move before your children complete this semester of school, but we can solve your problem by offering June 15th possession; and by putting your home on the market now, we won't miss out on any buyers presently in the market. Another thing you must consider is that it will take several weeks, at least, to find a buyer and secure the financing. If you want to move in early summer, your home should be on the market right now to insure that it will be sold by the time you need to move."

Another objection they may offer for putting their home on the market immediately is that repairs are needed.

Reply: "I certainly agree that it would enhance the sale of your home, Mr. Amos, but by delaying putting your property on the market you might lose the benefit you would gain from the repairs. Right now the market is good and money is plentiful. Before long, the market will be flooded with new listings which might tend to take the premium off of your home. And who knows what the mortgage market will look like in two months?

"Actually, these repairs could be made while we are arranging for the advertising and prospecting for interested buyers, couldn't they? If for some reason they are not completed when we show the home, we can point out to the buyer what will be done prior to the closing."

Objection 3: We are thinking about listing our home with Corona Realty.

Reply: "Corona is a good real estate firm. By listing your home with me, they and every other office in town will be invited to show and sell your home, but there will be one important difference. I can offer you personal service they can't, and you will have the advantage of knowing your listing agent is looking out for your interests."

Objection 4: We don't want to put our home on the market until we find another home we like.

Reply: "I realize your dilemma, Mr. Snyder. It is one faced by buyers every day. In fact, most of my clients have the same problem; but, on the other hand, can you afford to buy a new home without first selling this one?

"If it makes you feel any better, I can tell you that in over ten years of selling real estate, I've never had to move a seller out into the street. We have to be able to time the sale of your present home and the purchase of a new one so they coincide as closely as possible. The only way you can do that is to give your home exposure on the market while you're looking for another house. We can always arrange a possession date to insure that you have a home to move into.

"The opposite side is that you find a home you want, but aren't in a position to buy it because you don't have an offer on your present home. Then, while you try to sell your home, you take the risk of someone else buying that home. I'm sure you wouldn't want that to happen, would you?"

Objection 5: We are going to try to sell it ourselves first.

Reply: "Mr. Sawyer, I don't blame you for trying to save the real estate commission, but have you considered what is involved? As I pointed out in my listing presentation, I can offer several services that you cannot provide yourself. Besides those services, consider the problems of always having to be available to show your home, the danger to your family, and the difficulty two principals have in negotiating an agreement.

"Forgetting the advantges we can offer you of qualified buyers, controlled showings, sales ability, financing know-how, buyer follow-up, knowledge of the legal aspects of transferring a home, and our usefulness in negotiating between you and the buyer—forgetting all of these reasons why we are able to insure a more satisfactory sale, I want you to consider just one thing. Buyers automatically deduct 7 percent from their offering price because they know you aren't paying a sales commission. That's why they look at your home— they want a bargain.

"Are you willing to give up your evenings and weekends, to be bothered at all hours, to hassle with financing, and to take the chance of having your home tied up with an insincere or unqualified buyer, just so the buyer can save money? Why should you do all of the work, and the buyer get all of the benefits? Wouldn't your sale be less complicated, and probably more profitable, by allowing me to handle the headaches?"

Objection 6: I have a couple of people looking at it right now. If they don't buy my home, I'll list it with you.

Reply: "That's fine, Mr. Alsip. I'll tell you what. Let's go ahead with your plans of putting your home on the market tonight, and exclude your prospects from the listing. If they do decide to purchase your home, you won't have to pay us a commission, and I'll even be happy to help with the details. At the same time, we can have your home on the market and take advantage of other buyers presently looking for a home such as yours. Who knows, once your buyers discover that you have put your home on the market, it may make them take some action. What are their names? I'll exclude them from the listing for a couple of weeks, to give them a chance to make you an offer."

Objection 7: I don't want to tie up my property that long. Would you take the listing for 30 days?

Reply: "One hundred and twenty days is our normal listing period, Mr. Adams. I'm sure you can understand why we need this amount of time. We are going to spend a lot of money and time to attract buyers to your home. The average length of time it takes to sell a home in this area is 73 days. Now there is every possibility that your home will sell sooner than this, but we have to make sure we have an opportunity to bring you an offer, once we have put forth this much effort. We want to sell your home as quickly as you do—make no mistake about it—because we don't get paid until we find you a buyer."

Objection 8: I won't list my home for less than $60,000.

Reply: "Mr. Allen, that is your decision to make, and I assure you we will work very hard to get that amount for you. But I do want you to understand that no matter what you and I think your home is worth, the buyers are the ones who really decide the value of your home. You can't get any more for your home than a buyer is willing to pay. Someone looking at your home will view it in comparison to similar homes on the market. If we want to attract them to your home, we have to compete with the rest of the market, and your Competitive Market Analysis showed us where your home should be priced to compete with other homes like yours.

"I certainly want you to get as much for your home as possible. In fact, that is my job. But I don't want you to miss out on a buyer because of the listing price. It's true you can always come down later if your home doesn't move at $60,000, but there is also the danger that if you don't take advantage of the buyers presently waiting for a home like yours to come on the market, a later reduction won't solve the psychological stigma that will have surrounded your home.

"It is your decision to make, but my professional opinion is that we should get as close as possible to your competitors. How about putting your home on the market at $58,500?"

Objection 9: I would like to sell my house and buy a home in the country, but I hate to give up my low interest rate on this mortgage.

Reply: "I can certainly understand your reluctance to give up a 6 percent mortgage, Mr. Fryer, but you may not be saving enough money to compensate for not enjoying the home in the country you want. Since your mortgage balance is low and your equity is high, you aren't really gaining much by keeping the loan. The actual difference in interest you would pay for the same amount of debt at the higher rate wouldn't amount to more than a few hundred dollars a year. You lose more than that on the depreciation on your car each year. It's certainly worth as much to you to enjoy the home you want as it is to drive the car you want, isn't it?"

Objection 10: Last week an agent from Village Realty said he could get me $68,500 for my home.

Reply: "Mr. Delaney, buyers determine how much you get for your home, not the real estate agents. All we can do is offer our opinion as to what buyers might be willing to pay. Sometimes agents will be overly optimistic about your home's value because of their desire to get your listing. I don't feel this is being of service to you and I don't think you do either. The Competitive Market Analysis on your home shows us what buyers have been paying for similar homes, doesn't it? Taking this into consideration, do you feel your home will bring $68,500?"

Before moving on, let's review a few *Don'ts* of handling objections from the sellers:

1. *Don't* feel compelled to overcome every objection.
2. *Don't* counter until you are sure of the position or reasoning of the seller.
3. *Don't* agree with the seller if he or she is wrong.
4. *Don't* argue with the seller.

5-7. *How One Indiana Office Uses Canvassing to Fill the Shelf with Inventory*

A successful broker friend of mine from central Indiana knew canvassing was the quickest and surest way to increase his listing inventory and keep his supply stocked with choice listings. The difficulty was getting his agents to take the time and energy to actually canvass. They seemed to always have a good excuse for not doing so. He was even having trouble getting the listing agents to canvass the immediate neighborhood when they took a new listing.

To combat the problem, Ed decided he wouldn't leave anything to chance. One week he implemented a new policy of group canvassing. After each home was seen on the morning of the house tours, the entire group would spread out in a two-block radius of the listing and canvass for ten minutes. The listing agent was given the time from when he or she took the listing, until the group toured the home, to canvass the area. If the agent didn't, the group canvassed, and he or she lost all rights to canvass exclusively in that neighborhood.

Ed also took a page out of Danny Cox's teachings and required his sales staff to meet one evening a week for one hour and group canvass by telephone. Since he had more agents than phone lines, he split his staff up into several one-hour shifts, and ran contests between them to see which could come up with the most listing appointments within their allotted time.

By forcing his agents to canvass, both in person and via the telephone, Ed was able to see his number of listings increase by 120 percent in the first month, and maintain a high level compared to his competition throughout the year. After the first month, he also met with less resistance from his sales staff, since their incomes also increased considerably after practicing continuous canvassing efforts.

5-8. *Controlling the Seller Until You Bring Him an Offer*

As I pointed out in Section 5-1, most problems with sellers and with keeping your agents hustling for listings comes from lack of communication between the listing agent and the seller. You, as sales manager, can solve these problems by instituting programs that require your agents to communicate with their sellers.

Program A: Prospect Showing Report. By utilizing this form religiously, your listing agent is forced to communicate with the seller at a time when the seller most wants to know what is happening—after his or her property has been shown. If the listing agent actually informs the seller of the buyer's response, he or she can also expect to get problems with the listing corrected. Sellers listen to buyer's concerns about their property.

Program B: Weekly Contacts. Your listing agents should be required to make a weekly contact with the seller informing him or her of the activity, or lack of activity on the property, what the listing agent is doing and specific plans the agent will implement in the near future. A report of each contact should be turned into you, so you can monitor the contacts and ensure they are made on a regular basis.

Program C: Re-tour the Listing. If a property has been listed for more than 60 days, schedule another visit to the home by all of your associates. This practice will offer two benefits. First, the sellers will know they are not forgotten, and that their home is important enough for you to take a second visit to remind the agents of the benefits the home has to offer. Second, a second tour may remind one or more of your agents of some aspect of the home they had forgotten, or bring to mind a new buyer with whom they are working.

In the long run, unhappy sellers hurt the agency more than the agent. Sellers will remember a bad experience with a real estate company and broadcast their experience to anyone who will listen, much longer than they will remember who the listing agent was that provided them with the poor service. Don't assume your agents are communicating with the sellers, or feel that keeping the sellers happy is the responsibility of the listing agent.

6

Doubling Your Salespeople's Commissions with High-Powered Showing Techniques

Why do some salespeople become huge successes selling real estate, earning thirty, forty, and fifty thousand dollars a year, while others occupy themselves earning eight, ten, twelve thousand dollars a year? You provide them the same motivation, the same listings, the same advertising, yet there is a difference, a difference that costs you, and the agent, thousands of dollars each year.

One of the reasons for such broad differences in salespeople's commissions is the technique used to show and close home-buying prospects. High producers have learned how to get inside their buyers, to know how to set up the close, when to close, and which technique will work. Million dollar salespeople have no fear of the buyer or rejection, because they know their prospect needs them and, without asking the question, they will never earn the commission.

Chapter Six takes you inside these high-powered salespeople and the techniques they use to generate more and bigger commission checks. You can easily help your salespeople double their commissions by showing them how to incorporate these proven, effective techniques into their sales personalities.

6-1. *Educating Your Salespeople on the Overall Process to Give Them the Psychological Advantage Over Their Prospects*

Using psychology to develop the relationship your agent wants and needs with buying prospects is not a con game. Nor does it require an agent to be a trained psychologist. Every day we are faced with countless opportunities to either succeed or fail with people, depending on how well we anticipate their personalities and their motivation. Everyone uses psychology, successfully or unsuccessfully, every time they come in contact with another individual. As salespeople, we are required to use a higher level of psychology, and one that is aimed at causing a specific, positive response. In other words, our livelihoods depend on our successful use of this all-important technique.

Psychologically preparing a prospect for a specific response begins from the first contact, continues throughout the relationship, and most importantly, must be natural and sincere. It is not uncommon for an agent to concentrate on closing techniques, or even showing techniques as his only psychological tools, but those who limit their efforts to these aspects of the selling process are often disappointed and frustrated by their lack of success.

To ensure that your salespeople begin developing trust and respect from their clients from the very first meeting, you must arm them with the ability to read a prospect's personality, take control of the relationship, and develop mini-closes from the very start. By beginning on a solid base, every client will turn into a buyer and a commission check. Following are guidelines your agents should follow throughout the showing process.

1. Take control early, without being demanding.
2. Let the prospects know early that you are only interested in their needs.
3. Inform the buyer that you can solve any problem.
4. Show dedication to them, but also that your time is valuable and tightly controlled.
5. Continually ask closing questions.
6. Listen more than you talk.
7. Educate the buyer to the point of ignorance.

8. Closely consider the homes to be shown and their order of viewing.

9. Overcome objections with closes.

10. Conclude the showing at the most salable part of the home.

6-2. *Selecting the Right Home for Viewing*

Your agents, not the buyers, must control which homes the prospects inspect and in which order the homes are to be viewed. One of the hardest, yet most important aspects of the showing process is limiting the homes seen only to those the buyers are both qualified to buy and would seriously consider owning. When buyers make the decision to purchase a new home, they have a tendency to want to see everything on the market. Homes not suited to their needs and abilities only confuse buyers and make an agent's job more difficult when they view the *right* home. There is an answer to this always existent problem that will not offend buyers and will always leave them respecting the agent.

"Mr. Andrews, we saw a lovely home when we were out the other night. It's on 18th St., and it has a Thomas Realty sign in front."

"We'd like to see it."

"Yes, Mrs. James, I know the home and you're right, it is a lovely property. However, I feel it would be a waste of your time to view the home since it doesn't meet several of your most important requirements. (Now list those items not included in this particular home.) I can include it on our schedule if you'd like, but I don't want to waste your time; unless, of course, you feel you may be willing to change your requirements to fit this house."

Of the homes your agents do select for inspection, they should know which the prospects will buy. It doesn't take psychic powers for a professional to know which property comes closest to meeting the needs and emotions of their buyers. This home should be scheduled for the conclusion of the tour, and compared favorably with two other homes.

The first home shown will match the buyers' requirements on paper, but a physical inspection will find the home far removed from the buyers' idea of their dream home. The second home on the tour will be closer to that perfect home, but will lack the charm, personality, and key features of the third.

Now, the prospect is getting concerned. Will they ever find the right home for them? This element of fear will be your agent's strongest closing tool. When the buyers finally see their dream home, they will be so relieved, so delighted, they will jump at the chance to buy it.

By making the differences in the homes so obvious, the agent doesn't have to take sides, or try to "sell" the buyers.

I once had a couple from Cincinnati call me looking for a small farm. They had been coming up almost every weekend for two years, searching for just the right property. I had just listed a farm that I knew would be perfect for them, but I also knew that anyone who had spent two years looking for a farm would not be easy to sell. Rather than show them the property immediately, I scheduled two other farms before showing them my listing. It was obvious they were disheartened after viewing the first two rural properties, and were anticipating another wasted weekend when we pulled into the third property.

As the inspection tour began to unfold, I could see the delight in their eyes. I listened as they planned the number of livestock they could put in the pasture and visualized themselves out in the field on a tractor. As the tour concluded, the wife turned to me and said, "This is perfect! Why didn't you show it to us first?" I could have told her that if I had, she would still be looking for a farm.

6-3. *Setting Up the Sale While Driving Between Properties*

There are many ways to mentally prepare buyers for making a decision while going from house to house. There are also several ways to ensure that your buyers don't sign the offer. Before we get into the successful techniques for preconditioning the buyers, let's review the *don'ts* of driving from property to property.

- *Don't* distract the buyers by discussing topics other than the property being viewed or about to be viewed.

- *Don't* talk *up* the next house to be viewed.
- *Don't* drive by other similar properties with "For Sale" signs.
- *Don't* drive through business districts or run down neighborhoods.
- *Don't* attempt to sell them the property they just inspected.
- *Don't* distract the buyers with your driving habits.

Assuming your agents refrain from practicing the six *don'ts* just listed, the following three techniques are proven methods for preconditioning the buyers to make the offer.

A. When the buyers enter the car, take a blank offer-to-purchase from the car seat and hand it to them. "When we find the right home, Mr. and Mrs. Buyer, this is the agreement we will use to secure the home for you. Why don't you review it while we are driving to the first home, and if you have any questions, I'll be happy to answer them."

B. "Mrs. Buyer, here is a pad and pencil. As we view each home, make notes of your likes and dislikes. Later, we can review each home without being confused by which house had certain features." After viewing a property, and on the way to the next, discuss the pros and cons of the property. Listen to the comments of the buyers concerning certain features. This is your best clue to finding a selling point or technique that will produce an offer on the last home.

C. *Give them the home, then take it back!* During your drive to the last home on your tour, build up the hopes of the buyers by telling them about those aspects of the home that will be the most appealing to them. As they also begin to talk positively about the home, lower the boom! Overemphasize those features that are going to concern the buyer. Don't wait for the buyers to inspect the property and tell you what is wrong with the home. When they do see the home, they will not be surprised or disappointed by what they find. They will look at ways they can easily overcome the problems, rather than use them as an obstacle to buying the home.

6-4. Ensuring the Best Mental Attitude While Showing the Home

The only concern on the buyers' minds must be the purchase of a new home. Their attitude must be conducive to making a buying decision. Your agents have the responsibility for ensuring that a positive mental attitude is present while inspecting the home. To reduce distractions that force buyers to think of something other than "buying," your agents should incorporate the following techniques into their showing process.

1. Always enter the home before the buyers. This avoids any problems with pets, dark houses, introductions, etc.
2. Turn on all lights before the buyers enter the room.
3. Always lead when steps are present. If a step is weak or cluttered, better that you suffer the consequences than the buyer.
4. Take responsibility for wandering children. If the buyer has to chase his or her kids or constantly be calling after them, his or her mind is going to be on getting out of the house rather than buying it.
5. Highlight romantic features of the home. Light the fireplace, turn the intercom-stereo on low, stop in the flower garden, have the air-conditioner running, etc.
6. Spray air freshner in vacant homes prior to showing.

6-5. Teaching Your Agents to Sell the Home, Not Just Show It

There is a difference between selling a home and showing a home. It is not a difference that is obvious to the buyers, but it is a difference that is obvious in the end result. An agent who merely escorts a prospect through the property, letting the buyer go their own way, explaining in detail, "This is the kitchen," is *showing* the home. If, by chance he gets an offer, it's because the buyer bought the home, not because the agent sold it to him.

What you say or don't say, your manner, the route the tour takes, are all selling techniques. A quick walk through by the buyers does not give them the advantage of learning and experiencing the features a particular home offers. While you want the buyers to feel they *bought* the home, you must *sell* it to them one step at a time.

Following is a list of selling techniques offered by some of America's greatest real estate salespeople:

6-5A. *Sell Benefits, Not Features*

People don't buy two-car garages—they buy the luxury of being able to park both of their cars inside every night. Buyers don't buy family rooms—they buy a warm, lazy fireplace before which they can enjoy the fun of playing with their children. They don't buy a formal dining room—they buy entertaining their friends and associates. An agent must constantly practice selling benefits. Each feature of a home offers a benefit to the buyers. Zero in on the benefit, since the buyers can see the features and there is nothing of significance you can add to what their eyes can see. You can, however, open their imagination by making them think in terms of what a particular feature can mean to them.

6-5B. *Don't Overcome Every Objection*

Buyers offer two types of objections; the soft objection and the hard objection. The soft objection is a smoke screen. It really isn't an objection at all, but rather the buyer looking for a reason not to buy the home. The hard objection, on the other hand, is a valid concern and one that an agent may or may not want to address. Before attempting to overcome the hard objection, make the buyer voice it twice. If it comes up a second time, your agent must confront the problem and resolve it in the buyer's mind.

Do not agree with an objection that is not valid. You understand a fear, but you do not agree with it. The agent must show the buyers they really need not be concerned with an invalid objection.

"I understand how you feel Mrs. Johnson, but you really do not have to be concerned about that problem with this home. There is a bus stop just two blocks away."

6-5C. *Sell Related Benefits*

When the buyer expresses pleasure with a benefit a certain feature in the home offers, reinforce that pleasure by pointing out a related benefit also offered by that feature.

Don't just agree with what the buyer says, but also give him another reason to buy the home.

"This bedroom will make a nice sewing room."

"Yes, Mrs. Walters, it certainly will, and it will also make a nice guest room when company comes for the weekend."

6-5D. Listen

Give the buyers an opportunity to tell you their likes and dislikes about the home. Discover who is on your side and give him or her an opportunity to sell the other on the home. A spouse can be much more persuasive than a salesperson. An agent can uncover the motives and emotions of the buyers and, as a result, design his closing strategies, simply by listening to what the buyers are saying.

6-5E. Ask Questions That Force Prospects to Express Their Thoughts

You can't overcome a non-verbalized objection. Nor can you use a particular feature as a selling tool, unless you know it is important to the buyers.

"How do you feel about oil heat, Mr. Myers?"

"What would you do with this room, Mrs. Arnold?"

"Do you spend much time in the yard, Mr. and Mrs. Wysong?"

6-6. Using Psychological Leverage in Concluding the Tour

If you have selected the right home, and if you have implemented the showing techniques described previously, you are now ready to write an offer. The buyers are favorably impressed with the home and are visualizing themselves living in it. This is where many agents fail. "What do I do now?"

Unfortunately, many pack up the buyers and take them back to the office or back to the buyers' home. Others put the buyers in their car and say, "Well, what do you think?"

The transition becomes too abrupt for most buyers to handle. They have lost the atmosphere and positive mental attitude given them by being in the home. They now become more concerned about monthly payments, the down payment, interest rates, the large step they are taking, and any inadequacies of the home. The agent has lost the single biggest motivator available to him: the feeling of living in and enjoying the home.

Not only does the agent need to keep the buyers in the home until they make a buying decision, he must also conclude the tour in the most psychologically attractive part of the home. People don't pay $60,000 for a bedroom or a garage. They pay $60,000 for a view, for atmosphere, for charm, for an evening by the pool, or for a style of living. Why, then, would an agent conclude the tour in the bedroom area, or the garage, or an unfinished basement? End the tour in the area of the home the prospects are going to buy: where they imagine themselves living. Allow them (help them, if necessary) to see themselves sitting by the fireplace, entertaining in the formal dining room, barbecuing in the back yard, or enjoying their finished basement. Now they are as mentally prepared to buy as you are to sell.

Many times, if you give the buyers the opportunity, they will themselves select the most psychologically advantageous area of the home in which to make the buying decision. They will be drawn to one particular feature of the home, and continually return to it. When you find them obviously attracted to an area of the home, wait for them there, planning your close while they make a second tour of the home.

6-7. *How Your Salespeople Can Get the Buyer to Ask to Make the Offer*

Ideally, the best closing technique is to get the buying prospect to ask how they can buy the home. Over 80 percent of my buyers ask me, "How can we buy it?" or "What do we do now?" or "What will the seller take?" This high percentage of "self-closes" isn't a matter of luck. I have preconditioned the buyers to respond when they find the right home, to recognize that they have found it, and to sell themselves on it. To reach the results I want, I implement the following steps in the showing process.

A. The first meeting is very important to your goal of conditioning the buyers to say "I want it!" when they see the home you have selected. This is when you educate the buyers as to what they want, what they can afford, and the limited market these two features leave. Buyers see hundreds of signs and ads. They know that most of these will not meet their needs, but they do not realize how few of them *will* meet their needs. They feel there are at least twenty to thirty homes that are just right for them. If an agent allows this attitude to continue, the buyers will not make a decision until they have seen twenty to thirty homes. I show my clients that, upon researching their requirements, there are actually only three to four homes on the market they can even consider. Realizing this fact, they understand that they must make a buying decision from among those three or four homes, rather than attempt to see every home on the market. They are now mentally prepared to purchase one of the homes I will be showing them tomorrow.

B. By scheduling the tour as described earlier, I have made it obvious to the buyers that the last home they see meets their requirements much better than the first two homes. There is no question in their minds which home they want, because I have carefully selected two homes and scheduled them in an order that shows off the third property.

C. I have been on their side during the tours of the first two homes. I pointed out flaws before they did. I agreed with their objections. I suggested what I would want done if I were to buy the home. They now know I am as concerned about the home they are going to buy as they are, and I'm not trying to hide anything.

Now we are in the third house, and the buyers are very relaxed with me. *We* are looking for a home. Now I am as positive and expressive as they are about the features, and more importantly, the benefits of this home.

> "Boy, I really like this family room. This will be great for enjoying time with Jim and Jody, won't it, Mr. and Mrs. Abrams?"

> "I'm really impressed with the care this home has had, aren't you, Mr. Abrams? It certainly won't take much work, will it?"

> "Here's the place for your pool table, Mr. Abrams."

> "These hardwood floors are just beautiful, aren't they, Mrs. Abrams?"

"It's unusual to find so many conveniences in this price home, Mrs. Abrams. They're sure going to make your job easier aren't they?"

Excitement is contagious. The buyers begin to imagine themselves enjoying the benefits of this home. And after all, I am the expert. I see homes every day. If I'm excited about a house, the buyers know it is a home they can be proud of and enjoy.

6-8. High-Powered Closing Techniques that Get the Buyers' Signature on an Offer-to-Purchase

Notice that I said *High-Powered,* not *High-Pressured.* There is a big difference. The most effective closing technique is the one that does not indicate to the buyer that you are selling them the property. You have to let the buyers buy the home. Following are examples of how your agents can close with proven, effective techniques that make the buying decision an easy one for their prospects.

6-8A. The Assumptive Close

If the buyers have been as excited about the home as the agent, and have agreed with the agent's mini-closes, this close is a natural. It does not require the buyers to make a buying decision because, in essence, they already have.

"Mr. Michaels, so we don't forget anything, before we leave let's jot down the items you'll want to stay with the home. Will you need the drapes?"

"Mrs. Michaels, the kitchen applicances really go well with this decor. Let's see if we can get them to leave them with the home, shall we?"

"Mr. & Mrs. Michaels, let's sit down here and figure out what your monthly payments are going to be. Now, how much do you want to put down?"

6-8B. The Order Book Close

The buyers have already seen the offer-to-purchase, so they are not afraid of it. Your agent has been carrying it during the tour, clipped to his listing book. While in the most salable part of the home, he simply unfolds the offer, takes out his pen, and says;

"Mr. Snyder, the sellers are offering possession 30 days after closing. Is that fine with you?"

"For your protection, I feel we should ask the sellers to provide a termite inspection, don't you?"

"Will you want title insurance, Mr. and Mrs. Snyder?"

"Write your name on this line the same way you want the deed to read."

"It's normal that the taxes be prorated to date of closing. Is that okay with you?"

6-8C. *The Question Close*

Ask and you shall receive. Don't ask and you'll starve to death. Salespeople must realize that buyers are going to buy a home. That is why they are looking. The agent is the expert and they need his or her assitance to make an intelligent buying decision. Don't be afraid to ask.

"Let's make the sellers an offer before someone else steals this home away from you, shall we?"

"I don't think there is any doubt which home best suits your needs, is there Mr. and Mrs. Hines?"

"Wouldn't you love to own this home, Mrs. Hines?"

"If we can get the sellers to accept your offer tonight, Mr. and Mrs. Hines, we can go to the bank tomorrow and be closed within ten days. That will put you in the home at just about the time you need to move, won't it?"

"I think you'll really be happy with this home, don't you?"

6-8D. *The Ben Franklin Close*

For those buyers who are still hesitant and need additional support for their buying decision, the Ben Franklin Close is very effective. The agent takes out a piece of paper and divides it with a line down the middle. On the left hand side he writes "Pros," while on the right hand side he writes "Cons."

"Mr. and Mrs. Dunnington, let's take a look at the pros and cons of this home. By getting them down on paper, you'll be able to consider all aspects of the home and make a decision based on facts."

Now help the buyers think of the positive aspects of the home. When they run out of ideas, suggest other aspects of the home they haven't considered. Once you have completed the "Pros," hand the paper and pen to the buyers and say, "Now let's consider those things about the home you don't like." *Shut up!* From here on, the buyers are on their own.

When they are finished, you take the paper back and say, "Okay, let's see—we have 22 items that you really like about the home, and 4 items that you would rather have different, is that right? Well, by putting your pros and cons down on paper, I think it's obvious that this home comes closer to being exactly what you want than any other home we've seen, don't you?"

6-9. *Showing Your Agents Why Objections Are Opportunities to Close*

Professional real estate salespeople are not afraid of objections, they welcome them. They know that if the buyer doesn't voice his objection, they can never overcome the concern the buyer feels. They also know that objections show interest, and can be used as excellent closing tools. If buyers are concerned about the monthly payment, the condition of the home, the distance from work, or making a buying decision right now, they must have an interest in the property or they wouldn't care about the other factors.

When buyers offer an objection, they are telling the agent that they need help in making a buying decision. They need support for their judgment. The more objections they offer, the closer they are to making a buying decision. In the buyer's own mind, once your agent has overcome their objection and given them a logical solution, they are free to purchase the home.

Use the following techniques in fielding objections and turning them into motives for buying.

A. Don't overcome objections the first time they are expressed.

B. Take the buyer's mind away from the objection and wait to see if it arises once again.

Object: "I really wanted a bigger yard."
  "Aren't these flowers pretty? They have eight different varieties, most of which come up every year."

Object: "I'd like to have a finished basement."
  "Did you notice that the basement has been sealed? It appears to be dry, doesn't it?"

C. Don't argue or try to prove the buyer wrong. Be understanding and point out options he or she hadn't considered.

D. Always follow an objection with a close. Don't just overcome an objection and wait for another one. Once you have countered the objection, use the agreement from the buyer as an indication of his or her desire to purchase the home. Go right back to another close.

E. If buyers were confident that their objection ruled out a home, they wouldn't bother to voice it. The buyers want to be shown why their concern need not stop them from owning the home they want. Don't make light of their objection or make them feel foolish for raising the question, but do show them how others with the same concern have handled the problem.

Object: "The home is priced too high for the repairs that are needed."
  "The home does need some repairs, Mr. McCracken, and the sellers took that into consideration when they put the home on the market. The other homes in this area are selling for $2,000 to $2,500 more than the offering price on this home. Actually, you can buy more house than you normally could, and you realize the increase in value by making the repairs, rather than if the present owner makes them. So, it's really to your advantage, isn't it?"

6-10. Two Reasons Why Real Estate Salespeople Fail in Their Attempt to Show Real Estate Successfully

If you accompany your salespeople on a showing, you will discover that two factors prevent success in all cases. These factors are self-imposed barriers that you can help your agents overcome. By watching closely and analyzing what happens during the showing process, you will be able to determine which factor is responsible for your agent's lack of success.

6-10A. Lack of Technique Knowledge

Obviously, some agents who fail just do not know how to show a home. They let the buyers take the lead; they point out obvious features, rather than expounding on the benefits; and they fail to watch for or recognize buying signals. The material contained in this chapter, along with your guidance, will overcome this obstacle for your agents. While experience is necessary to refine technique and succeed with the most difficult of clients, proper training will give your agents the basic knowledge and ability they need for success with 95 percent of their buying prospects.

6-10B. Lack of Proper Attitude

By proper attitude, I do not mean they must want to be successful or feel confident of their selling ability. Showing success depends on a different type of positive attitude. Let's stop and consider what your agents are really thinking when they're showing a home. First, there is a fear of rejection. They don't want to seem too aggressive or high-pressured. Second, they are not confident of their closing ability and are wondering how they can close at just the right time. Third, they have been conditioned since childhood to believe that every buyer is wary of salespeople. Because we emphasize the need to overcome buyers' objections, our salepeople begin to think all buyers in every situation are opposed to a buying decision and are just waiting for the agent to make his or her move. The first two problems with attitude are easily overcome, and are ones that you, as sales manager, often discuss with your salespeople. Seldom, however, do sales managers really look inside the heads of their salespeople and attempt to change this biggest attitude problem.

Do you have a salesperson who works very hard, makes all of the contacts he or she should, studies every piece of training material, yet can never seem to be as successful as someone with these ingredients should be? Of course you do! Let's get inside the head of that salesperson, and by understanding what may not be obvious, find a means of improving how the agent feels about him- or herself.

From the time the agent was a child, he or she has been conditioned to be wary of salespeople. Parents, teachers, television, and bad experiences with salespeople selling questionable products have taught him or her that salespeople want to sell you something you really don't want to buy. The agent was educated to believe that you must take everything a salesperson says with a grain of salt. When he or she began a real estate selling career, the first thing we concentrated on teaching was how to convince buyers and sellers to work with him or her, without them knowing they were being sold. This agent's outlook is much like that of a policeman who went into his career wanting to help the innocent and rehabilitate the guilty, but was soon so involved with criminals that he began looking upon all people as being bad.

Likewise, this salesperson has adopted an attitude that all buyers and sellers do not trust him or her, really don't want to buy the product, and will reject him or her if trying to close. What else can the agent think? We tell him or her to be positive—that success is a state of mind, and then proceed to concentrate all of our training on the negative aspects of selling real estate.

How can you help this salesperson to change this attitude? Simply by taking the time to make the agent consider the product, the service, and the needs of the client. I have no fear of knocking on doors. I have no fear of asking a seller to list his or her home with me. I have no fear of asking a caller for his or her name. I have no fear of asking a buyer to make an offer. I have not overcome these fears because I am successful; rather, I have been successful because I overcame these fears. Note these ideas:

1. I sell a product of which I am very proud. I have absolutely nothing to apologize for.

2. My prospects need my product. They cannot survive without it.

3. I provide a service that not only contributes to their happiness, but also protects them from losing money through lack of knowledge.

4. I am the best. Buyers and sellers are fortunate to have me as their agent, because I will protect them, arrange the financing terms they need, and use all of my expertise to their benefit.

5. They came to me because they needed my guidance. If I do not ask them to buy or make them consider every reason they should buy, I have failed them.

6. I'm not selling anything. I'm showing them the opportunity to buy what they want.

These six segments are all true. No salesperson or buyer can question these facts. Put together, they construct the attitude necessary for successful selling. The only obstacle between your salespeople and their adoption of this attitude is that they have never really sat down and considered what their duties really were. They have dwelt on the negative and not the positive. Sure, we have to be armed with techniques to overcome objections, to close without seeming to pressure, and to get our foot in the door, but not because the prospect doesn't want or need our service or a particular home; rather, it's to give them an opportunity to consider factors that, without us, they could not consider.

7

Writing
Advertising
That Returns $$$$$

Writing effective, result-oriented advertising is a key to the success of every real estate office. Much more of an office's budget is allotted to advertising than any other expenditure; yet little formal training is available for the sales manager who is responsible for this all-important marketing function. The result is that most advertising is uncreative and poorly designed. Advertising becomes a matter of highlighting a few features the ad writer feels are attractive in the home, and utilizing as many medias used by other offices as financially possible.

Chapter Seven reveals proven advertising techniques that also reduce cost and increase response. Your advertising will become more creative and effective if you follow these useful suggestions. You'll learn how to better utilize every advertising media available to you, how to write more exciting copy that will make the phone ring sixty, seventy, even one hundred times a week, and how to design a more successful advertising campaign overall. You'll find examples of how advertising directed at particular groups paid off and how to use "Attention Getters" in your headlines. Your ads will contain fresh ideas and life, they will be noticed, and the phones will begin to ring, more than ever before.

7-1. Pinpointing the Results You Want from Your Advertising Efforts

Before you can write a successful ad, you must first determine the purpose of the ad, for whom you're writing the ad, and the response you want to generate from it. Whether you're using line ads, picture ads, radio, television, sign, billboard, pamphlets, or institutional advertising, you must direct your copy toward the specific response you want to generate, which eventually boils down to making the telephone ring.

While your specific goals may differ, the following results are those that your ads should be designed to generate:

A. *Newspaper Line and Photo Ads*—Make the reader pick up the phone and call your office right now.

B. *Open House Ads*—Make the reader get in his or her car and visit the property.

C. *Billboards, Institutional Advertising, Television and Radio Advertising*—Create awareness of your office, so your name will be in the forefront of buyers' and sellers' minds when they think real estate. You also are preconditioning the public's attitude, so your salespeople will be received more readily.

D. *Signs and Inserts*—Develop awareness that (1) the property is for sale and your office has the listing, and of (2) your activity, by the number of signs spread throughout the community.

These goals are hard enough to fulfill, without further complicating them by trying to sell the property in your ad. The purpose of writing an ad is to get the phone to ring, to give your salespeople an opportunity to do what they do best. That's it! You can't get the buyer's signature through an ad, so don't try to sell the home in one paragraph.

Another important goal when writing an ad is to generate as many calls as possible that can be shifted to other listings. To ensure that your ads pull double duty, make your copy general enough to fit several homes in a specific price range. (We will review examples of how you can write this type of ad in Section 7-2.) If a reader needs four bedrooms, or a specific location, an ad proclaiming three bedrooms or another location would not make the prospect pick up the telephone. Since you know you have a home, or can find one that fits a buyer's needs, you need not be concerned with trying to attract *the* buyer for a particular home from a specific ad.

7-2. *Writing Advertising that Cuts Costs and Increases Response*

Now that you have defined your goals, you can take steps to refine and improve them by breaking them down even further. You don't just want the phone to ring, you also want it to ring often and decrease the cost of making the buttons light up. There are several ways to make both of these secondary goals happen.

First, as I mentioned briefly in the preceding section, you can use a shotgun approach with your ads. By directing them at more than one category of buyer, you can run fewer ads and also increase the number of floor duty calls received. If you list specifics of a home, you eliminate prospects who require different qualifications. By making the home attractive to several types of buyers, you give your salespeople an opportunity to use their skills to introduce the caller to just the type of home they desire.

You have several homes in the $80,000 price range. They have a few similar features, so you capitalize on them to generate calls from buyers in the $80,000 price range using just one ad. They do not have the same location, number of bedrooms, size of lot or type of construction, yet you will give enough details to make every $80,000 prospect feel they have found the home for which they have been looking. Here's a sample of just such an ad.

> **Superior Interior**
> **Enjoy gracious living in this rustic family home. Offers wall-to-wall carpeting, central air, formal dining room, and family room with stone fireplace. If you insist on excellence, call Bob Thorman today on this $80,000 dream house with assumable mortgage.**

Another method of reducing your advertising costs is to put more emphasis on widely distributed weekly newspapers. In our community, we have a weekly paper that delivers free copies each Wednesday to every door in every town or city in the county. This paper is closely read by every family, mainly because of the "Garage Sale" and "For Sale" ads it contains. We found that we could run two full pages of picture ads each week for one fifth the cost of running classified or line ads in the larger, more commercial daily paper. Not only does the weekly have greater readership because of its delivery system, but also, all readers see the pictures of our homes, not just those who are looking for a home and turn to the classified section. Our response increased substantially when we reassigned the main thrust of our advertising, and our sellers were pleased that a picture of their home appeared twice a month in the newspaper.

Other methods of reducing your advertising costs per home sold or listed, while increasing the number of responses per advertising dollar spent, include handouts, billboards, brochures, and inserts. We will discuss their advantages and the proven techniques employed in using each of these methods later in this chapter.

7-3. Creating a Successful Newspaper Ad

Good, effective advertising copy is not written, it is created. You construct it with the same care, professionalism and result-oriented techniques that you use to create effective sales and listing presentations. In Section 7-8, you will discover what professional ad writers look for in an ad and the responses you must generate with your ad copy, but for now let's concern ourselves with the mechanics of creating successful newspaper ads.

There are ten steps to building good ad copy. Each is as important as the next, and all must be present if you are to receive the maximum response from your advertising dollar.

7-3A. Ten Steps of Successful Ad Copy

1. Know the property well. If you are to utilize the key selling points offered by a home, you must be familiar with the property. Why would someone want this home? What advantages does it offer over other homes? What was the deciding factor that made the present owners purchase this particular home?

2. Know your intended audience. Determine the type of buyer most likely to be best suited for this home, and then emphasize those aspects that are most likely to catch his or her attention. Put yourself in the place of the buyer. What would make you pick up the phone and call?

3. Keep your copy simple. Don't confuse the reader or make the copy so difficult to follow that more effort goes into reading the ad than writing it. Use motivating, powerful phrases. The shorter the sentences the better. And make your copy smooth and easy to read.

4. People buy with emotion, not logic. Make your ads emotional, not logical. Generate positive emotion within the reader by concentrating on the same emotion that stirs in buyers when they decide to purchase a home. Since the buyer can't see the property in the ad, you have to use words to develop a mental picture that will force him or her to respond. Use phrases such as:

Delightful	Striking
Majestic trees	Relaxed
Elegant formal dining	Quiet setting
Tranquil	Graceful
Lavish	Large country kitchen
Unique	Kid-Oriented
Warm wood paneling	Spacious
Country setting	Spectacular stone fireplace
Tree-studded	Warm and friendly

5. Write for the buyer, not yourself. You are not writing the ad for the seller, your salespeople, your competition, or yourself. You are writing it for the buyer. Watch carefully your use of abbreviations, business slang, or points that are important only to someone in the real estate business. Read your ad out loud. (Your reader will.) How does it sound when spoken? Have you used phrases that stir emotion and promote response?

6. Write for response, not space. Too often, ad writers concern themselves more with the length of the ad than its content. Tell your story, as powerfully and effectively as possible, and stop. If it's two lines, fine. If it's ten lines, great. You want calls, not neat-looking copy. And re-

member, you're not selling the home in the paper, so don't try. Keep your ads crisp and brief.

7. Motivate your readers. Get them excited. Imagine a reader, looking up from the paper and shouting to his or her spouse in another room, "Hey, Hon, listen to this one!" Use words that motivate and demand action. "New," "Hurry," "Last Chance," "Quick," "Discover," "Now," "You," "Family," and "How To" are all words that will motivate your reader. Use action words that get the wheels turning and the fingers dialing.

8. Eliminate cliches. Newspaper ads on homes, cars, televisions, lipstick, and wigs are filled with "Won't Last," "Call Today," "Just What You've Been Looking For" and "Best Price In Town." Buyers don't take these words seriously anymore. They are knowledgeable today and are not influenced by trite phrases and tired cliches.

9. Use the truth to your advantage. If you have exaggerated the home in your ad, the buyers will be disappointed when they see it. Just because your ads have to be truthful, however, doesn't mean you shouldn't capitalize on the truth. Accent features such as handyman specials by making the property sound worse than it really is, or by listing the types of trees and plants to be found, or by conducting a verbal tour of the property.

10. Write your ads in advance. Most sales managers are constantly haunted by their advertising deadline. Fast copy, however, is seldom good copy, and is never the best copy. Your ads should be written at least two days prior to your deadline. After being away from it for a day, review your ads. Do they still appeal to you? Do you feel that they still have as much impact or convey the message you intended? I know of no author, speaker, or teacher that submits their first copy on their subject. They write it, come back after a short period and rewrite it, and may even rewrite it again before they are satisfied with their product. Why then, if professionals, who make their living from the written word, can't do their best work the first time, do sales managers think they can write successful, phone-ringing ad copy in just one sitting?

7-4. *Using Radio and Television to Ensure a Positive Response for Your Agents*

Yes, continued television and radio advertising is expensive. But used properly, it need not be as expensive as you might think, and the results can be extremely beneficial to your agents and your office. As I mentioned earlier, television and radio advertising should be used as institutional advertising. Its purpose is to make the buying and selling public aware of your office and the special services you have to offer. No one is going to hear or see your commercial and immediately pick up the telephone and call you. If that is your only goal, don't use these media.

Over a period of time, however, you will create an awareness of your firm and develop a public image that will make buyers and sellers think of you when they decide to sell or purchase a home. Your agents will be met with greater acceptance because they represent a company the public has been exposed to and recognizes. Every day, you see commercials on television or hear them on the radio advertising products or services. The intention of these advertisers is to make you so familiar with their merchandise that, when you are ready to buy or when you're at the store, you automatically think of their product. Very few commercials are designed to motivate the audience to take immediate action and those are mail order businesses.

Since developing public awareness of your firm is a steady process of shaping buyers' and seller's attitudes over a period of time, you will have difficulty pinpointing the results of your efforts or seeing an immediate improvement in sales volume. You must gauge the success of your commercials over a period of months and compare them with advertising dollars allotted to the radio and television media. You will also find that these media are too expensive to use on a day-to-day basis. To take advantage of maximum exposure, yet keep your cost to a minimum, implement the following guidelines into your television and radio campaigns.

1. Design your ads for 15- or 30-second spots, rather than one-minute ads.

2. Commit to a long term contract to reduce the cost per ad.

3. Rather than running your spots four or five times a day,

run them only once a day, with rotating slot times every second day.

4. If possible, sponsor a real estate consumer spot like a "Tip of the Day," advice on real estate questions, etc. You may even be able to host the segment yourself.

5. Remember the purpose of your ads. You want to plant a seed in the buyer's or seller's mind. Repeat your firm's name often, at least four times in each ad. The longer the spot, the more often you can use your office's name.

6. Be consistent. Keep your name in front of the public on a regular basis.

7. Develop a theme. Give the audience something that catches their attention and leaves an impression on them. You are developing your image as well as the community's attitude towards your company. Examples of strategies other offices have used effectively include: 6 percent commission rate in a 7 percent market, guaranteed sales program, length of service in the community, volume of business, national contacts, industry contacts, or any other feature you have to offer. Continue to hit upon your theme. If you have a catchy slogan, fine; use it. But a slogan, just for the sake of having a slogan, isn't necessary.

7-5. *Five Guidelines to Successful Institutional Advertising*

Scorecards, placemats, menus, guidebooks, pens, calendars, matches, and playing cards can all be methods of utilizing institutional advertising to increase your exposure to the public. The purpose of this form of advertising is to reach people you ordinarily wouldn't have a chance to contact and make aware of your firm's services. Once again, remember that the purpose of institutional advertising is to familiarize potential buyers and sellers with your firm, not for them to immediately pick up the phone and call you.

Before I discuss the use of institutional advertising, I want to take a moment to discuss how *not* to use this technique. We are constantly deluged with opportunities to buy handout items such as key chains, pens, bottle openers, calendars, etc. Even though your competitors use these items, for the most part, they are the most ineffective use of your advertising dollar possible. If you get close enough to a prospect to hand him or her matches, a pen, or a calendar, he or she already knows of your firm. In fact, except for when canvassing, the prospect is familiar enough with your agent or your office because he or she has been in contact with you. What, then, is the advantage or benefit to be gained by handing this prospect or client a book of matches or a pen? In other words, the distribution of your handout and who receives the gift is more important than the gift itself.

A good example of institutional advertising is the use of scorecards at a miniture golf course. The owner has to provide each group of players with a card to keep track of the score, but the card itself is an expense for the owner, rather than an income producer. The owner has no need to advertise on the card, since by the time it's handed out, he or she already has the customer. You can utilize this opportunity, however, by buying the scorecards for the owner and including your ad at the bottom or back of the card. This will save the operator money, and will give you an inexpensive means of reaching thousands of new prospects. You can use this same technique with restaurant menus and mats, bowling score-sheets, signs at Little League ballparks, moving company brochures, etc.

Following are the five keys to effective institutional advertising,

1. Choose a business that attracts the type of people most likely to buy or sell a property.
2. Limit your advertising to businesses that get local trade or patronage from those who are considering a move into your community.
3. Stay away from items that contain advertising from several other businesses.
4. Negotiate for the best location possible on the item for your ad.
5. Take the order to the printer yourself. This allows you to compare rates, approve copy, and to also make another contact at the same time.

7-6. *How Institutional Advertising Has Worked for Others*

Many offices have put their creativity into institutional advertising campaigns. Following are some examples of institutional advertising used throughout the country.

1. *Garage Sale Signs*—These signs have proven to be extremely effective since the entire population of this country seems to be hooked on garage sales and visits them regularly.

2. *Billboards*—Billboard advertising has been proven effective when combined with a slogan or central theme that is easy to remember. The same advertisement should be placed at the same time, on at least three billboards in different locations around the community.

3. *Builder's Brochures*—Real estate firms that have put together and paid for brochures for builders have reaped the benefits by reserving the back page for their own advertisement. This is an excellent method of reaching both buyers and sellers.

4. *Flyers from Lumber Companies, Home Improvement Stores and Furniture Stores*—I know of several offices that have received a very good response by paying for flyers mailed out by these types of other business establishments, in return for a small ad in the flyer.

5. *Restaurant Place Mats*—This type of institutional advertising works well for two reasons. First, your ad is seen by a large number of people from a broad range of income brackets. Second, with service being what it often is, the customer has ample time to read your message.

7-7. Using Inserts for the "Hard-to-Reach" Market

Inserts bring to mind two different methods of advertising. One is the simple matter of placing an insert in your "For Sale" or "Sold" sign, while the other is a more complicated process of including one- or two-page printed paper inserts in with the delivery of the daily or weekly newspaper. Since both are a form of advertising, and each can be very effective, we will take a look at how to use either or both methods to your advantage.

7-7A. Sign Inserts

All salespeople are aware that the "For Sale" sign is the most effective method of advertising available. It's inexpensive and catches the attention of neighbors, buyers presently in the market, and people driving by the property. The use of inserts can increase the effectiveness of this form of advertising even more. Inserts in signs are an excellent way to zero in on particular buyers and make them take special notice of the property. My most successful inserts include, "G.I., No Money Down," "Duplex," "Basement," and "Contract Terms Available." Other inserts can also be effective: "Four Bedrooms," "Family Room," "Immediate Possession" and "FHA Terms Available."

The use of inserts gives you that extra opportunity to catch the attention of someone who has been looking for a particular feature, and who thinks of this home solely because that feature is present.

7-7B. *Newspaper Inserts*

A two-page insert includes typesetting, photographs, and printing, and can be produced for about $75 per thousand copies, with even lower costs per thousand as the quantity of your order increases. Newspaper carriers or newspapers themselves will put your inserts in their paper or deliver it with their paper for as little as two or three cents each. This gives you an opportunity to hit those hard-to-reach prospects, and give them an inexpensive, two-page presentation.

If you want to reach apartment dwellers, design your insert to address this type of buyer and contract with carriers who deliver to apartment complexes. If you want to pursue listings in a particular area, concentrate your attentions on those sellers. Your inserts can be anything you want them to be, and can be directed toward any group you want. Inserts are the most flexible form of advertising for the money invested.

7-8. *How Professional Ad Writers Judge the Criteria a Successful Ad Must Meet*

Professional ad writers and advertising executives use a four-part criteria when judging the potential of ad copy. Whether the product is real estate or steel doors, all four elements must be present if an ad is going to be successful. Compare your ads with this formula. Do they meet each criteria? If they don't, you aren't making the phone ring as often as it should, and could.

A. Attract Attention
B. Create Interest
C. Build Desire
D. Encourage Action

7-8A. *Attention*

Something within your ad, usually the heading, must attract the attention of the reader. Your heading may seem to contain this quality when alone on your desk, but when it reaches the paper, it will have to compete with hundreds of ads. Don't take your headings lightly. Judge them as though they were in the middle of a hundred other ads.

7-8B. *Interest*

Now that you have their attention, your ad must hold the interest of the reader. Again, remember that the prospect is browsing the paper for potential homes. He or she will not read every ad, and those that lose his or her interest, even for a second, will lose the reader forever.

7-8C. *Desire*

Interest becomes desire. Build up the reader. Make the reader visualize him- or herself in the home, living in the house. Use motivating phrases, descriptive words. Concentrate on emotion, not four walls and carpet. When prospects visualize a home, they don't see a certain number of bedrooms, baths, or room sizes. They see plush carpeting, comfortable living, cozy fireplaces, and flowering trees.

7-8D. *Action*

If they don't pick up the phone, your ad has failed. You must create urgency, promise their dream home, and then threaten to take it away if they don't take positive action immediately. Give just enough details to make the reader thirst for more.

Each of these goals can only be met one way—with words. Don't take the easy or quick way out. Don't settle for tired phrases. Be creative. Make your ad different, as well as desirable. Rodales' *The Word Finder* and *Roget's Thesaurus* are two excellent guides to refreshing and descriptive uses of the English language. If you want to say "bright," these two references will provide you with various words and phrases to help you be more descriptive and motivating, such as sunny, rosy, cheerful, shiny, etc.

The only thing wrong with stealing an idea is stealing a bad one. When you see creative advertising, regardless of the product, borrow the technique and incorporate it into your ads. Some of my best ads come from material completely unrelated to real estate sales. There is no copyright on good ideas.

7-9. *Designing an "Overall" Advertising Campaign*

If you follow advertising and firms that are successful, you find they all have one thing in common. They have a predesigned, consistent advertising campaign. They use a central theme throughout their medias, whether television, radio, newspaper, billboard, or magazine. They intentionally want to be recognized for a particular characteristic and they project the same image with all of their promotions. Only over a long period of time do they change their direction, but when they do make a change, it is made throughout their campaign.

How does this strategy compare with your advertising efforts last year? Did you know the direction you wanted to take and design every method of advertising you used to complement each? If not, the following formula will help you put together an advertising program that will bring you the same local recognition as Sears, Xerox, Pepsi, or McDonald's.

1. *Determine Your Goal*—When the buying public thinks of you, what feature do you want to come to mind? Professionalism? Friendliness? Large size? Conservativeness? Guaranteed Sales Programs? Neighborhood Specializa-

tion? Set your goal and build your campaign to present the image you want.

2. *Use a variety of medias*—We are all limited to some extent by our advertising budget. Still, you must distribute your advertising capital to as many medias as possible to ensure that you are reaching all segments of the market.

3. *Be different*—Don't be flaky, and certainly not unprofessional, but do develop medias or techniques that will ensure that you stand out from your competitors.

4. *Keep Your Theme Simple*—Remember: your goal is recognition. Don't try to educate the public on every facet of your operation.

5. *Make a Total Commitment*—Your entire method of doing business, your agents, and your attitude must be tied to your advertising campaign.

7-10 *The Effect a Creative Change in Advertising Has Had on Other Offices*

Over a period of years, offices have a tendency to automatically accept a philosophy of advertising without taking a close look at new techniques. They become stale and develop an image of a second-rate office. To break out of this slump, you must implement new and creative themes in your advertising program. Once you have established your new program, you can change it slowly and consistently with the market and your success; but to break out of your rut and be noticed, you need radical changes in your campaign. Two such examples of offices introducing creative changes in this program to raise their level of competitiveness follow:

Faced with declining volume and the introduction of two new offices in the community, this Arizona broker decided he had to change his entire method of operation, including advertising, if he was to maintain the position he had worked so hard to reach. His new direction was quick, pre-planned and drastic, including:

A. Remodeling the interior and exterior of his office building.

B. Attracting new blood by promising a total commitment to

his salespeople and offering fringe benefits such as: draws, insurance, bonuses, and office space.

C. Reducing his commission rate and using the lower rate as his central advertising theme.

D. Utilizing new medias such as radio, weekly papers, billboards, and institutional advertising.

The results were extremely positive, with a gross increase of 122 percent in office earnings in the first year.

After purchasing an existing, unproductive office, this broker elected to institute less drastic, but equally effective changes in his office's image through his advertising campaign. He immediately

A. Sponsored a contest in the local paper for students to develop a new slogan for his office.

B. Promised sellers that every listing would be advertised each week.

C. Implemented radio advertising, sponsoring local sports programs.

D. Doubled his advertising space to four pages in the biweekly "Homes" magazine of the multi-list service.

Within six months, his office had become the third largest office in the area and the second largest in number of listings.

Neither of these brokers' advertising material was particularly creative. The success they enjoyed was not due as much to what their advertising message contained as it was to the fact that they both made changes and developed their advertising around those changes. They were noticed because their campaign was new and fresh, and was easily recognized by the buying public.

7-11. *How You Can Keep the Telephone Ringing with Your Advertising Efforts*

If your phone is going to ring often, your advertising must meet the four-step formula for successful ads. Writing good ad copy and keeping your floor duty agents busy is not difficult. It does require that you give special attention to your ad copy, though. Following are examples of creative, phone-ringing ads that meet all four criteria: attention, interest, desire, and action:

EXECUTIVES. Here is a home that sets the standard of living you want. Four-year-old ranch with beautiful stone exterior and an interior you'll be proud to entertain in. Five bedrooms, large living room with fireplace, formal dining room opening onto patio, full basement with stone fireplace, 3 full baths, game room. All nestled on 3 wooded acres with detached 2½ car garage. This country beauty is priced at $75,000.

AN ACRE IN THE CITY. Located Northeast near University, this home offers extra living quarters for your live-in relatives. Enjoy having mom with you in her own apartment. Large lot for gardening and children.

HEARD A GOOD TWO-STORY LATELY? Well if this one could talk, it would tell you about the loving care it has received over the years. Or, it might tell you what a good southeast location it has to offer, or how its 6 large rooms and 2 full baths can make your family enjoy its style of living. Make an appointment today to take a listen and a look at this low 50's home.

CONTRACT BUYERS. Home on Northwest side that owner will consider a contract on with $3,000 down. Total price of $35,000 leaves room for you to do decorating and a little remodeling. If you have more energy than money, call today for an appointment. Immediate possession.

IF YOU CAN AFFORD THE BEST, this ad is intended for you. One of Centerville's finest homes, this beautiful stone ranch has been owned by the same family since it was nine months old, and the love and care shows up throughout. 1,800 square feet of living luxury, plus full finished basement. If it's time for that final move up, call about this elegant home before it's too late. Priced at $95,400.

95.7 ACRES. One of the prettiest small farms in the county. Sharp farmhouse offers hardwood floors, electric heat, fireplace, and country kitchen. Large 36 × 51 barn in excellent condition, 300-bushel and 500-bushel corn cribs, hog shelter, oat bin, 2 chicken houses, and good fences. Woods, pastures, and highly productive, tillable ground.

FHA-VA BUYERS. We have several homes available under FHA-VA financing. VA buyers need no down payment and FHA buyers need only 3% down. Right now the interest rate is good and we have many sellers willing to pay all costs. If you have been wanting to buy but were unable to get someone to help, call us today.

7-12. Using "Attention Grabbers" in Your Headlines

The heading is the most important segment of your ad, since if you don't catch the eye of the reader, he or she won't read the ad. Following are examples of excellent, proven "Attention Grabber" headlines that have made the phones ring at real estate offices in the past.

Singing in the Kitchen

Heard a Good Two-Story Lately?

I Belong to a Two-House Family

It Is and It Ain't

$4.00 Monthly Payment

Raise Your Own T-Bones

Hey, the Dude's Buying

Superior Interior

Somebody Missed the Boat

Country Living

Quiet Setting

Stop Making the Mortgage Payments

Economy Model

I Hope You're Hard to Please

Kids Grow, Apartments Don't

Have to Move Quick?

The key to your successful heading is to be able to say the same thing in a different way. While "Assumable Loan," "Contract," "5 Acres," "Four Bedrooms," and "Full Basement" are all what the buyers are looking for in a home, they are also the same headings being used by every real estate office in the country. Put the same heading beside them, and you have given the reader no reason to take notice of your ad. It is normal to think that, since you are putting so much effort into writing your ad and paying so much for it, every prospect will also read it. You are close to your ad, and to you it is the only one in the paper, but readers—home buyers—do not single out your ads. You have to make them take notice by making your ad jump out and grab their attention.

7-13. Creating and Using Handouts that Generate Positive Responses

Handouts are badly neglected by real estate offices. They have been used as the primary advertising media of department stores, groceries, furniture stores, and other retailers successfully, yet real estate brokers have failed to catch on to how to use them to their benefit. Handouts enable you to reach a specific market and enlarge upon your message, giving you more space and time to give a complete sales presentation, thereby reducing your cost of generating clients. *All* handouts are not effective, however. You can easily break your advertising budget using handouts that only pay off for the company that sold them to you. Following are some guidelines for the successful use of both product and printed handout advertising.

7-13A. Product Handouts

Much use is made of handout products such as pens, key chains, matches, calendars, etc. in our industry. The majority of this advertising is ineffective and expensive. As I pointed out earlier, if you are close enough to hand the gift to the prospect, you don't need the gift. The result is that the people who end up possessing your give-a-way items are friends, customers, or people who stop by your office on their own. What new customer's have you generated through the use of product handouts lately?

You can, however, make certain items work for you.

1. *Matches*—Distribute boxes of your matches to other businesses in exchange for theirs. You will be reaching new customers by capitalizing on their customers; customers you might otherwise have never reached. You can also put your advertising dollar to good use by placing your matches in cafeterias and offices of local industries.

2. *Telephone Dial Markers*—Dial markers that glow in the dark are useful items that make good handouts because your prospects see the product several times every day and it is an item they can use. It can also be easily included in an envelope for mail canvassing.

3. *Hurricane, Fire, or First Aid Action List*—These products are useful and will be displayed by the receiver, again putting your name before them on a daily basis.

4. *Metric Conversion Tables*—With more weights and measures converting to a metric measure, most adults find themselves unfamiliar with the new system. These charts are helpful and appreciated.

As important as your selection of product handouts is, your method of distribution is even more important. To be effective, they must get into the hands of new contacts. This can only be accomplished through distribution by personal canvassing or placement in other local businesses. You will never make a sale by giving friends, clients or customers items such as key chains, pens, or calendars.

7-13B. Information Handouts

This type of handout is the most effective of the two, since it enables you to inexpensively put two, four, or six pages of ad copy in the hands of a prospect. These can be distributed personally door-to-door, by mail, or inserted in a newspaper. Obviously, the most effective use is personal, door-to-door distribution. Following are the three types of printed material proven effective in generating a response:

Current Listings—Include photos and details of your most attractive listings. This can be a simple one-page handout, printed on two sides, or a brochure of 12 or 16 pages including financing information, etc.

Listing Presentation—As an aid in getting your foot in the door, develop a two-page pamphlet on why sellers should list their home with a real estate office, and specifically, your office. A good local printer can help you with format, style, and color.

Information Packets—Most abstract companies will be happy to supply you with brochures on title insurance, why sellers should use a professional agent, legalities of selling a home, etc. They cost you nothing and provide your agents with something to put in a prospect's hand when they open the door.

7-14. Establishing a Realistic and Successful Advertising Budget

The percentage of income you allot to your advertising budget will vary, depending on your volume of sales, the competition and the number of salespeople associated with your office. The larger and more successful your office, the smaller the percentage applied to advertising. The real key, however, is know-ing where to draw the line between spending more than will be returned. In other words, merely spending large sums of money on advertising won't produce more sales. There is a point where additional advertising no longer means additional volume, or cer-tainly profit. Making the smartest, most productive use of your advertising dollar will enable you to keep your percentage in line, regardless of your office size.

A realistic advertising budget is 20–23 percent of gross in-come. It is difficult, if not impossible to get under this amount, and if you are spending more than 23 percent, you are not generating the volume of business you should be from your advertising ef-forts. Your advertising budget is broken down in six areas.

1. Newspaper Daily Classified   60%
2. Open House Ads   15%
3. Institutional Advertising   8%
4. Radio and Television   10%
5. Handouts   3%
6. Signs   4%

Break your budget down even further by computing the ac-tual dollars per month you will commit to each type of advertising. Don't be afraid to cut back on your advertising space or frequency. Many successful offices have found they can stretch their advertis-ing dollars by advertising in Sunday classifieds only, dropping unproductive institutional advertising and putting out their own listing magazine rather than advertise heavily in multi-list bro-chures.

Once your budget is established, you should meet with your salespeople and review the new budget and allotments with them. Seek their ideas and help in creating a successful advertising pro-gram. Also point out to them the cost of each call they receive and the importance of making the contact productive. Many offices have carried control of the advertising budget a step further. They allot each agent an amount equal to 10 percent of his or her monthly commission for advertising listings. If the agent exceeds this amount, he or she is responsible for the difference. This policy encourages the agent to write better ads, and make his or her listings more salable.

Regardless of the allotment system you use, to ensure that your advertising dollars are well spent, you have to impress upon your salespeople the commitment you make on their behalf in terms of dollars, and the commitment you expect from them in return.

8

Establishing
Office Policies
That Encourage Success

No person, no team, no business can be successful without direction and discipline. Whether self-imposed or provided through leadership, direction and discipline are essential to sustained success. As sales manager, you can provide both of these to your salespeople by implementing a workable office policy. While we all realize that we must have certain rules to live by and conduct our business, seldom do we consider that these rules can and should be propellants to creativity, aggressiveness, and success for both the individual and the office.

Chapter Eight presents you with a policy structure that puts life into your office and develops the opportunities for your salespeople to utilize their talents to make them and your office "Number One." Through the use of motivating and useful guidelines for all parties, your policy will encourage an attitude and atmosphere that ensures success.

8-1. *Success Is a State of Mind You Can Develop for Your Salespeople*

Success is not a factual or mechanical measurement, but rather an attitude, a state of mind. Success must be in your salespeople's environment, in everything and everyone with whom they come in contact. It begins with your method of operation and the manner in which you conduct your business. Your office policy is your tool for planting in your salespeople the seed of being a winner.

While you use many such tools as motivation, training, and office image to instill a successful attitude in your salespeople, no instrument is more important to your purpose than the guidelines you set that dictate how your agents will conduct themselves. You can use all of the motivational techniques you want, but if your operation doesn't suggest success by presenting itself as a first-class operation, your salespeople will conduct themselves as second-class agents. There is a theory that everyone wants discipline. Whether you agree with that reasoning or not, people have come to expect discipline as well as leadership. If it isn't present, you and your office will lose the respect necessary to make agents believe they are associated with a successful office.

Real estate salespeople have a preconceived image of what a successful office should be. Part of that image is the office policy they expect to live by. If your office policy doesn't encourage them to operate in a successful manner, they won't. It's that simple.

8-2. *Establishing Office Policies that Will Achieve Your Objectives And Create an Atmosphere of a Successful, Well-Organized Office*

Your office policy should not be designed solely for control and the benefit of the office. Only if your policies provide incentive, freedom, and motivation for your agents will they also make your office successful. A fair office policy will establish discipline and direction for both the office and the agent, while, at the same time, making it easier and more enjoyable to earn a good living with your office.

Chapter Three (3-3) discussed the ingredients and presentation of a successful office policy handbook. The guidelines are presented clearly, in a manner that motivates, rather than inhibits. When establishing an office policy, you should ask yourself the following questions:

A. Is the policy needed?

B. Is it one-sided?

C. Is the policy too dictatorial?

D. Does the policy motivate or inhibit creativity?

Since you may have policies other than those given you in Chapter Three, let's consider which policies are motivating and which are inhibitive.

8-2A. *Motivating Office Policies*

1. Equal commission split between the selling and the listing agent
2. Floor duty
3. Supplies, forms, advertising furnished by the office
4. Telephone usage
5. Sales meetings
6. Record keeping, registering offers, changes, and forms
7. Dress
8. Sales manager assistance, handling of disputes, etc.
9. Client and prospect control

8-2B. *Inhibiting Office Policy*

1. Larger than 40 percent office share of the total commission
2. Requiring salespeople to be in the office at a certain time each morning
3. Limits on telephone use
4. Limitations on the area or type of transaction
5. Long periods of floor duty, rather than two- or three-hour periods at intervals throughout the week
6. Demands on the salesperson's time

Real estate salespeople are unique. They have different personalities, drives, and types of creativity than any other category of professional I know. Your office policy must address this uniqueness and control it, without subduing it. These characteristics must be encouraged, not restricted, since they are what make a few people in this world great, rather than just good.

8-3. Developing Standards of Operation

A must within all large industrial operations, real estate offices can also benefit from written "Standards of Operation." As part of your office policy, this document is a written procedure that states how a duty is to be performed, and which duties are expected of each individual. It eliminates mistakes and poor communication, and ensures that the proper practice is being followed at all times. Your "Standards of Operation" should cover the following areas:

A. Responsibility of the Listing Agent

B. Responsibility of the Selling Agent

C. Responsibility of the Floor Duty Agent

D. Responsibility of the Showing Agent

Each area covered should include the following details:

A. Timing—When is the duty to be performed?

B. Location—What area is to be covered, where is the information to be recorded, etc.

C. Step-by-Step Instructions—Inform the agent what is to be done first, second, third, etc.

D. How—If there is any room for doubt, list specifics of technique, dialog, etc.

Your "Standard of Operation" should discuss all areas of responsibility, including: turning in a listing with all pertinent information, advertising copy, signs, keys, recording and presenting offers, communications, the closing process, meetings, problem-solving, legal work, and floor duty techniques. These written procedures will prove extremely valuable as you employ new agents. While you may explain certain procedures and responsibilities to your new people, it is easy for them to forget key points, since they are being deluged with information in a very short period of time.

8-4. Improving Communication to Increase Sales

Communication is vital to the success of any business, as well as the long term success of the individual. Your office policy must encourage, in fact demand, two-way communication. While this fact may seem obvious, my visits to real estate offices of both large and small staffs have made me realize how little emphasis is placed on communication within the office. I find most systems cumbersome, causing delays of several days in communicating pertinent facts to salespeople within their own office.

Following is a list of areas that must receive immediate and clear communication between salespeople if each is to earn his or her maximum potential in real estate sales.

8-4A. *Offer-Book*

As important as offers on property are, I find many offices have developed systems that reduce the number of offers they might receive, as well as competition to sell a listing. If the fact that an offer has been received is not communicated to all salespeople, you have disregarded an excellent method of motivation and increased your chances of difficulties. You have also created a problem once the offer is accepted by not having an easy, quick method of informing your other agents.

An "Offer Book" makes communication better and competition keener. A three-ring, looseleaf binder is placed on the floor duty desk. The page is divided with the following headings:

Date	Property Address	Selling Agent	Listing Agent	Date Presented	Accept	Reject	Price	Terms

When an agent obtains an offer, he or she immediately records it by completing the first four columns. The listing agent is required to check the book *before* presenting the offer, and record the time and date he or she is going to present it to the sellers. If any other offers come in prior to that time, the agent, of course, must present all offers at the same time. After presenting the offer, the agent records the information by completing the remaining columns in the "Offer Book."

All agents should check the offer book each time they enter the office or call for messages. If a property is placed back on the market, the listing agent is required to record it in tne "Offer Book" immediately, so that all agents will know the property is available. There are three big advantages to your office by using this method of communication:

1. Every agent knows the status of every property at all times.

2. It acts as an incentive to obtain another offer before the first offer is presented.

3. The book becomes a motivator, since agents will check the book to see how they are faring each month, as compared to the other agents in your office.

8-4B. *Changes on Listings*

There are often changes affecting listings that need to be communicated to all of your salespeople. A "Change Book," which is simply a notebook, should also be left on the floor duty desk, to be checked each day by all salespersons. Information to be recorded includes new phone numbers; changes in tenants, possession, and occupancy; reduced prices; new terms; items changed from the original listing; the extention of listing; and any other information that will enable your agents to be as knowledgeable as necessary to sell the property.

8-4C. *Sign Book*

All salespeople should record the address of a property when they place a sign on it, along with the date it was installed and the date picked up. Selling agents should also record placement of "Sold" signs and the date these are picked up and returned to the office.

8-4D. *Forms*

Forms should be utilized as a means of communication between your salespeople and yourself. The following forms are of special importance in improving communications. (Copies of these forms are available in Chapter Nine.)

1. Property Showing Report—All sellers (and listing agents) want to know what the buyer's response was when the property was shown. The selling agent completes the form and gives it to the listing agent, who passes the information on to the sellers.

2. Closing Progress Report—Each party to the transaction will know the status of the pending closing at all times if this report is updated daily.

3. Listing Evaluation Form—A simple, quick method of

> providing the listing agent with a consensus of his or
> her listing and comments, if needed, to use when
> discussing needed adjustments with the seller.

The implementation of these policies and forms must be office-wide if they are to be effective. These four steps will ensure communication within your office and eliminate problems and inefficiencies generated by poor communicative techniques.

8-5. *Creating Uniformity of Conducting Business*

With few exceptions, your top producers must conduct their business in the same manner as your lowest producers. In regard to office policy there can be no exceptions, no privileges. You cannot allow one agent to work under a different set of rules from the remainder of your staff, unless you want your office to soon consist of one salesperson. Even worse than the threat of losing the support of your other agents is the fact that once an agent, even a good one, realizes he or she can control you, his or her sales begin slipping, as does the agent's respect for your office. Uniqueness, individuality, and creativity can be tolerated. Mavericks cannot. Nothing is worse for morale than for your salespeople to see someone work outside the boundaries within which they must work.

All of your agents must be given the same opportunities to succeed. They must feel that they are as important to you as your top producer. Remember, nobody is more important then the team.

8-6. *Guidelines for Preventing Disputes*

One of your first goals for your office policy is the prevention of disputes among your salespeople. Disputes are demoralizing, time consuming and always unproductive. You can have as much impact on their prevention as on their solution. The guidelines you choose and the communication of them will set the type of competitive spirit present in your office.

Your office policy handbook should include specific coverage of this all-important subject. Disputes arise 90 percent of the time because of a lack of consideration for others. These are the 90 percent you can eliminate by addressing the five major areas of controversy:

A. When is a client a client?

B. What are the responsibilities once a particular agent has been requested?

C. What is the commission split for referrals or when one agent must handle another agent's client?

D. What is the procedure for presenting offers?

E. When is a client no longer a client?

You can only prevent questionable actions by building mutual respect among your sales staff, but you can eliminate obviously unethical practices by answering the above question in your office policy manual. The best prevention of future disputes is the action you take on the first dispute to arise. If you are firm and swift with your disciplining, your decision will serve as a deterrent to others. If you are hesitant to take action, you will be encouraging future misconduct.

Some disputes are honest. These should be discussed by you and the salespeople involved. Once you have listened to both sides, give the parties an opportunity to work out their own solution. If, for some reason, they are still unable to agree, you must become Solomon and issue a judgment that is not only fair, but also does not cost you one of the salespeople.

8-7. *Maintaining Control of Your Staff*

Sales managers are constantly faced with the problem of controlling their staff without losing them. It is not an easy tightrope, but you must walk it or face failure on either side if you fall. Controlling salespeople, like motivating them, requires you to look at your agents as individuals. What works with Janice probably won't work with Bill. While you must use the same guidelines and rules for everyone, how you make the agents conform to those rules and remain productive must be designed according to the traits of each individual.

Following is a list of personality types and the best means for controlling each. The majority of your offenders will fall into one of these categories:

Over-Aggressive—This person has good intentions and a big ego. Point out his or her errors gently but firmly.

Non-Motivated—Find this person's motivating factor and develop it. Once motivated, he or she will fall into line.

Inexperienced—Be patient. Explain the need for certain rules and how they have enabled others to succeed.

Know-It-All—Give them an opportunity to lead, no matter how small the role. As a role model, they will fall into the mold you want.

Non-Comformist—Let this person know you respect individuality, but for the morale of others, he or she must adhere to certain guidelines.

Unorganized—Give them a system and show them the importance of planning. Start with small schedules, such as putting aside an hour a day to canvass or making fifteen phone calls a day. Once they see the benefits, they will be more inclined to working under a strict schedule.

Selfish—This individual's concern is "me." Make it clear that "me" is in trouble if he or she doesn't fall in line. Self-interest will bring him or her around.

8-8. *Areas an Effective Office Policy Should Cover*

Your office policy need not be exactly like my example in 3-3. Multiple branches, different area practices, and the size of the operation may dictate a difference from the policy handbook I have developed. Regardless of differing circumstances, however, there are certain basic areas your handbook must address, since organization is as important to an office as it is to an agent. Written guidelines eliminate the need for decisions—tough decisions—at a later date. Eliminating decisions means eliminating the chance of making a mistake or allowing poor morale to develop.

To ensure that you sidestep these problems, your handbook must include your policies on:

A. Commission Splits

B. Taking Property Off the Active Market

C. Presenting Simultaneous Offers

D. Placement of and Responsibility for Signs

   E. Updating Pending Files and Progress Reports
   F. Floor Duty Assignments and Procedures
   G. Participation of Managers
   H. Tour of Homes
    I. "Whose Client"
    J. Writing and Placement of Ads
   K. Income Requirements
   L. Attendance and Participation at Sales Meetings
   M. Open Houses
   N. Canvassing and/or Farm System

8-8A. Commission Splits

Spell out your commission splits for each type of transaction including selling agent, listing agent, cooperative sales, VA and FHA repossessions, referrals, etc. The common practice within your area will naturally weigh heavily in determining your schedule, but don't be afraid to be creative if your schedule will be more motivating. You should also list the rates you charge for each type of property and your minimum fee.

8-8B. Taking Property Off the Active Market

Sellers do change their minds and their circumstances. If it is your policy to remove a property from inventory when requested by the owners, indicate so in your manual, along with the conditions that must be present, the procedure to follow, and any obligation on the part of the owner.

8-8C. Presenting Simultaneous Offers

Even though law requires that all offers made on a property be presented, your handbook should spell out the responsibility of the listing agent and the procedure to be followed.

8-8D. Placement of and Responsibility for Signs

Step-by-step, list the duties of the listing agent in putting up a "For Sale" sign, recording it in the "Sign Book" and returning the sign if the listing expires. Any charges for lost or damaged signs should also be listed, as well as the procedures and responsibility of the selling agent in placing, removing, and returning "Sold" signs.

8-8E. *Updating Pending Files and Progress Reports*

Include in your policy manual instructions for keeping pending files and progress reports up-to-date. Describe when information must be recorded, what information is needed, and who is responsible for recording different steps of the closing process.

8-8F. *Floor Duty Assignments and Procedures*

Discuss who is expected to take floor duty, how often the agent will be assigned floor duty, and how floor duty is assigned. Your instructions should also include the responsibility of the floor duty agent, arrangements for trading floor duty assignments with another agent, and the importance of following up on calls properly.

8-8G. *Participation of Managers*

Tell the agent what he can expect from his sales manager, what the sales manager can do for him, and the relationship between the agent and the sales manager concerning noncompetitiveness, confidentiality, personal problems, etc.

8-8H. *Tour of Homes*

Specify the day and time of your tour of homes and the participation expected by all agents. If listing agents have particular responsibilities during tours of their listings, make certain it is so noted, along with any practice concerning the immediate neighborhood after securing the listing.

8-8I. *"Whose Client"*

Address the five questions I gave you in Section 8-6. Emphasize a matter-of-fact style enough in this discussion so that your agents have no doubt as to what is expected of them when a situation of this type arises.

8-8J. *Writing and Placement of Ads*

Make your agents aware of your advertising policies. Who writes the ad, when they write it, what is the frequency of advertising on each home, who pays for the advertising, and what types of advertising can they anticipate are all questions your manual should answer.

8-8K. *Income Requirements*

If you require a minimum level of production from your salespeople, indicate the amount in the manual. You should also include time frames for new agents to reach the minimum level and what the agent should do if his income is not up to par.

8-8L. *Attendance and Participation at Sales Meetings*

As with the "Tour of Homes," specify the day and time of the sales meeting, the importance of attending it and what will happen there, particularly anything requiring the direct participation of the agent.

8-8M. *Open House*

Your discussion of open houses will cover five areas:

A. Statement of support of Open Houses

B. Expected frequency of Open Houses

C. Responsibility of ad copy

D. When the sign is to be put up and canvassing of the neighborhood

E. Whom (within the office) to contact for approval of the Open House

8-8N. *Canvassing and/or Farm System*

If you expect or require canvassing by your agents, a statement should be included here. If you assign farm areas, explain your system as well as how canvassing is to be conducted.

8-9. *Keeping Flexibility In Your Office Policy*

If nothing else, my kids have taught me that two old adages are still very true: (1) Rules were made to be broken, and (2) Times change. Your rules cannot be rigid or permanent. You must be able to use common sense when situations arise that cause an agent to bend the rules. You must also stay in tune with modern philosophies and changes in the manner of doing business within your industry.

The least painless way to adapt or bend is to write your policies in a tone that suggests rather than demands. You can put together a set of policies that establishes guidelines and gets your point across without backing yourself into a corner by making flat, concrete statements. Notice that my policy handbook in Section 3-3 uses phrases such as:

". . . should dress."

"You are an independent . . . , not an employee."

". . . your personal choice."

"Your attendance is imperative."

"To ensure . . ."

"We recommend . . ."

"To assist you . . .

By using these terms and showing the agent that these policies work for him or her too, the manual does not lay down the Ten Commandments, but rather, offers a discussion of office philosophy and the preferred manner of doing business. The tone you use is important if your agents are to feel your policies are both flexible and motivating.

8-10. Putting Your Policy Manual into Booklet Form

Physically putting together a policy manual can be very easy and as expensive or inexpensive as you desire. Cost really comes down to the type of binder, using a copy machine versus a printer, and typing versus typesetting. For offices of less than one hundred agents, typing the pages and copying them on your office copier is the least expensive. If more than one hundred copies will be distributed, typesetting and copying by a printer are more attractive and become financially feasible.

Following are three tips for the physical make-up of your manual:

A. *Binder*—Select a three-ring binder, similar to the size used for your listing book. This will allow easy insertion of new material. Put the agent's name on the front of the binder with a plastic imprinter.

B. *Pages*—Only discuss one subject on each page. Then, if

you make a change, only that subject must be retyped and replaced. If replacement pages exceed the original ones, you can use a secondary numbering system, such as; 25A, 25B, etc.

C. *Indexing*—Don't! Each change will require a new index. Your manual won't be so large that the reader will have difficulty locating a particular section.

After the introduction, there is no "best" order of arranging your material. You can become as extravagant as you want with your manual by using binders imprinted with your company logo and name, using company colors, and breaking up different areas of discussion with dividers. While you need not go to these lengths, it is important that your manual look neat, professional, and official. A sloppily compiled booklet will bring doubt as to the professionalism of its content as well.

8-11. *Introducing New Procedures to Your Salespeople*

You can never forget that your salespeople are buyers, just as much as real estate prospects are buyers. If they are not sold on an idea, they won't be enthused about it. You have to use the same process on them as you would on anyone else you wanted a particular reaction from.

Don't inform them of new policy. Discuss *need* and *solution.* Explain why it is good for them, not you. Solicit comments so you can have an opportunity to overcome their objections, rather than have them build up inside the agent. Treat your agents as you would any other prospect and, most of all, show respect, both in the policy itself and in the manner by which you introduce it.

8-12. *Why Successful Offices Have Well-Structured and Controlled Office Policies*

I could end this chapter with two words: *Morale* and *Control.* Successful offices implement specific office polices for two reasons only. You encourage your agents to work in a professional manner and within the framework you have established to enable you to control your agents, rather than your agents controlling you. By conducting your business in a professional manner and avoiding disputes, you also keep your agents' morale high. Without control of your agents and high morale among your staff, the techniques you use for motivating and training, no matter how creative, cannot succeed.

9

Using Forms
To Increase
Communications and Sales

Real estate salespeople, and even a few sales managers, feel that being required to complete forms and records only takes away from their selling time and produces nothing in return. History has proven this isn't true, and except for those cases in which sales managers go overboard and bog down their salespeople with forms, they can be extremely productive. While it is true that for unsuccessful salespeople, forms are a glaring admission of non-productive habits, successful real estate professionals know the value of forms and records in their businesses, and rely on them for guidance and reminders.

Chapter Nine shows you proven, effective forms that increase communication and motivation. You will see how they assist the agent in keeping track of clients, in constantly using the proper formats, and in assessing how his or her time is best spent.

9-1. Recognizing the Importance of Using Sales-Oriented Forms

It's true that forms are often more valuable to you as sales manager than they are to the salesperson, since they tell you how hard the agent is working, how productive this person makes his or her time, and where the agent is succeeding or failing. They can also tell the salesperson the same thing, but without your reviewing

165

and discussing them with the agent, he or she is likely to pass up the information in favor of continuing bad habits. The agent may not be able to see what he or she is doing wrong, unless you point it out. For these reasons, the forms in this chapter have been designed to be your indicators of how to increase the productivity of your agents.

The importance of these forms lies in their ability to help the agent use proven formats in different situations, so he or she can concentrate on new prospects, communicate with clients and associates, and aid you and him- or herself in diagnosing what can be done to increase sales and better utilize available time. Putting his or her activities into a form that can be easily reviewed and evaluated can make the agent more aware of his or her strengths and weaknesses.

9-2. *Defining What You Want a Form to Do for You and Your Salespeople*

On the remaining pages of this chapter, you are given samples of fifteen proven, sales-oriented forms and discussion of how each should be used to help your agents generate sales. When considering if your office should put these forms into your system or whether to design other forms for your agents use, you must first define what you want the form to accomplish, and then evaluate how effective the form will be in reaching the goal you have set.

Go through the following steps when considering if a form will be helpful to you and your salespeople, and what it should contain to bring about the desired results:

1. What do I want to accomplish?
2. Can the form be completed in a few minutes?
3. Does the form infringe upon the agents' professionalism, right to clients' privacy, or integrity?
4. Can I accomplish what I want without the form?
5. Can I show the agent how it will help *his* or *her* business?
6. Is it as streamlined as I can make it?
7. Have I left anything out that would make it a better, more effective form?

Try the form out yourself for a short period before you introduce it to your salespeople. Ask for your agents' ideas on what forms would be helpful to them. Are there any formats that you can put together from proven techniques such as listing presentations, interviews, etc., that would be effective for them? Don't be afraid to steal successful ideas from others. Improve upon them and incorporate them into your system. I am never ashamed to learn from the successes of others in order to increase my own success. It's when I borrow their failures that I become upset with myself.

9-3. Seventeen Effective Forms that Help You Foresee Problems, Evaluate Trends, and Supervise Salespeople

How you utilize these forms and how the salesperson uses them will often be quite different. For the most part, they are your indicator of activity, productivity, and effectiveness. To your agents they are records, formats, and a means of communication. We will discuss them, of course, from your point of view, and how you can use them to help the salesperson and evaluate his or her performance. With each of the seventeen forms presented on the following pages, we will review how to instruct your salespeople on their use, and how you will use them to help your agents overcome any problems they are having.

These are all actual forms compiled from the most successful offices in the real estate business. They have proven themselves to be sales-generating and informative. Our checklist includes:

Offer to Purchase

Listing Agreement

Prospect Showing Report

Housing Requirement Analysis

Telephone Inquiry Sheet

Daily Schedule

Competitive Market Analysis

Closing Progress Report and Pending File

Monthly Income Record

Daily Worksheet Report

Prospect Data Card

Detailed Listing Card

Advertising Analysis

Closing Record, Year-to-Date

Salespeople's Commission Record

Goal Form

Listing Evaluation Form

9-4. Offer-to-Purchase

To an agent, an offer-to-purchase is the goal he or she has worked for up to this point. To a buyer, it is a legal contract that will bind him or her to a decision, even if it is a bad one. To overcome this feeling, the agent must make the offer a selling tool, rather than an instrument of fear.

In real estate school, your agents learned how to legally complete this document, but they learned nothing about the psychology of using it as a selling tool and eliminating the buyers' fears that are brought on by the agent's producing it. There are several small, but subtle techniques your agents can use to change the offer from an obstacle to an aid.

By following these simple rules, your agents will find that the offer is much better received when it is time for the buyer to put his or her name on the dotted line.

1. Have an offer-to-purchase on the car seat next to you when your clients get into the car. On the way to the first showing, hand it to them with the following comment:

   "This is a copy of the agreement you will be okaying when we find the right home for you. Take a minute and look it over now. If you have any questions, I'll be happy to answer them."

   You have accomplished several goals with this gesture: you have told them you expect them to buy a home from you. You are not out for the ride. You have also made them more comfortable with the form. They will not feel the need to read over every line when you get to that big moment. Finally, you will not have to be worried about when to spring the offer on them. It will always be in plain view.

2. *Never, never* use the words *"contract"* or *"sign."* They sound legal, binding, everlasting. They put fear into the hearts of buyers and sellers. "If you'll just okay the agreement here, we'll see what we can get the seller to do." It's warmer, it's easier, it's less final.

3. Fill in the listed price, unless the buyers have indicated another price. You can always fill out a new offer if they object so strongly that you can't overcome it. If you don't put in the listed price, you don't know what to put in the blank without the buyers making a "take-action" decision.

4. Review Chapter Six for other techniques involving the offer-to-purchase.

9-5. Listing Agreement

Again, you must help the salesperson differentiate between what was learned in a real estate course concerning the legal requirements of a listing agreement and the requirements for getting a salable listing.

Your agent should accomplish several goals with the listing form.

1. It should contain all of the information necessary to answer the buyer's questions.

2. All information contained should be accurate and verified.

3. It should be motivating to the salespeople not only from your office, but also from other offices. Include highlights of the property and those points that the seller has appreciated most about the home over the years.

4. Your advertising people should be able to write effective, result-getting ads from the information contained. Make sure the agent gives them material to work with.

5. The questions you ask when completing the form should be leading to the sellers' signatures on the listing agreement. Each time the seller answers a question, you are one step closer to getting the listing approved.

6. Review Chapter Five for other techniques of getting the sellers' signatures on the listing agreement.

9-6. *Property Showing Report*

The "Property Showing Report" in Figure 9-1 is extremely simple, but serves many purposes. First, it ensures good communication between the showing agent, the listing agent, and the seller. The listing agent will know what the prospects thought of the property, and can use the information not only to keep the sellers informed, but also to help prepare them to do something to their property to make it more marketable if need be, such as making repairs, lowering the price, offering terms, etc.

You can gain much more from the showing reports. They are indicators of how many properties an agent is showing, how many of these are to the same client, why his or her clients are not buying the homes shown them and why the listing isn't moving. If you find that the selling agent is showing many homes to one buyer, you can work with him or her to determine why he or she hasn't received an offer. If the agent's activity is low (few showing reports), you can review the reasons why he or she isn't showing more property. You will also use the forms to work with the listing agents to aid them in getting changes made in a listing that isn't moving.

While the form asks for the name of the buying prospect, don't make this a requirement if the selling agent has a fear of giving out the client's name. Ask the agent, instead, to assign numbers to his or her clients. Either way, you will have the information you need from this form.

9-7. *Housing Requirement Analysis*

This form will better enable both the agent and the prospect to envision what the buyers are really looking for, what they need, and what they might settle for in a home. When your agents are using this form, it is important as part of their selling technique that they don't become order takers or interviewers. Their attention should be on the buyers and not on the form. If they are familiar with the form prior to using it, they will be able to ask the necessary questions and jot down the answers without constantly looking at the form. Introducing the form is an easy and effective way to get the buying prospects to open up and begin thinking positively about purchasing a home.

```
┌─────────────────────────────────────────────────────────┐
│  Whalen Real Estate                                       │
│                                                           │
│              PROPERTY SHOWING REPORT                      │
│                                                           │
│  TO: _____  │
│               (LISTING SALESMAN)                          │
│                                                           │
│  PROPERTY: _____  │
│                                                           │
│  DATE SHOWN: _____  │
│                                                           │
│  PROSPECT: _____  │
│                                                           │
│  COMMENTS: _____  │
│  _____  │
│  _____  │
│  _____  │
│  _____  │
│  _____  │
│  _____  │
│                                                           │
│                      _____  │
│                           (SELLING SALESMAN)              │
│  ---------------------------------------------------------│
│  TO: Salesmanager                                         │
│  I have discussed the above showing with the property     │
│  owner.                                                    │
│                                                           │
│                      _____  │
│                           (LISTING SALESMAN)              │
│                                                           │
│                      _____  │
│                                (DATE)                     │
└─────────────────────────────────────────────────────────┘
```

Courtesy of Booher & Day

Figure 9-1

"Mr. and Mrs. Buyer, to make sure that we are looking at the right type of homes, let's take a minute to jot down your requirements in a home. That way I can concentrate on finding the right one for you and not waste your time on homes that don't meet your needs."

As a sales manager, you can use this form to determine if your agents are prepared, know what their clients are looking for, and are possibly letting their clients waste their time on unrealistic requirements. (See Figure 9-2.)

HOUSING REQUIREMENT ANALYSIS
(Client Interview Form)

Name _____ Address _____
City _____ Home Phone _____ Bus. Phone _____
Number & Ages of children _____ Pos. Required _____
Price Range _____ Down Payment _____ Financing _____

	First Choice	Second Choice
Style of Home		
Location Desired		
School District		
Bedrooms		
Family Room		
Basement		
Garage		
Den		
Dining Room		
Type of Heating		
Fireplace		
No. of Baths		
Eat-In Kitchen		

Special Requirements _____

_____

_____

Comments _____

_____

_____

Figure 9-2

9-8. Telephone Inquiry Sheet

This carefully constructed and proven successful format is a tremendous aid to your salespeople on floor duty. Followed correctly, it will enable them to enjoy a large percentage of productive calls while on floor duty. They should be well rehearsed in the use of the form so the caller will not realize they are using a pre-designed format. (See Figure 9-3.)

As a format, it enables the floor duty agent to get the lead he or she needs from the caller. As a record, it tells to whom he or she has talked and what the prospect is looking for in a home. As sales manager, you will learn how effective the agent is on the floor and how well he or she is following up on leads. Each phone call that comes in on floor duty is costing you between $10.00 and $30.00, depending on the number of calls and your advertising budget. You must turn them into commissions if you are to realize a return on dollars invested. Have your floor duty agents complete this form in duplicate with carbon paper, leaving you the copies and keeping the original for follow-up. During your monthly individual meeting with the agent, he or she should report to you the results of this follow-up as you evaluate the agents floor duty techniques.

9-9. Daily Schedule

Since new agents will not have had exposure to working unsupervised, and previously unproductive agents obviously have not used their time wisely, great care should be taken to explain not only the use of this form, but also the importance of utilizing their time wisely. All agents should spend the early morning hours before they leave home considering how they are going to spend the rest of their day. Once they get into the field, selling should be their only concern, not wondering what else they have to do today. Utilizing early morning hours for this saves precious time for selling. (See Figure 9-4.)

Every detail that requires their attention during the day should be put on their schedule, no matter how minute the detail might be. Their priorities should be listed in order of importance, and the highest completed before moving on to the next item. They may not complete all of their priorities today, but what they do complete will be the most important and the most profitable.

TELEPHONE INQUIRY SHEET

Whalen Real Estate   Make every prospect call count

      To be used by salesman on every prospect call. Use the following format:

Answer: Good morning, Whalen Real Estate, Mr. _____
speaking. May I help you?

Customer inquires on   (particular house)

(Ad) _____ (Sign) _____ (Other) _____

Answer: "YES, I'll be glad to assist you. Just a moment and I'll get the record on that and give you the information. (Pause) What is your name? _____
and your phone, Mr. _____ _____
                                        (Phone No.)

AREA
1. Are you familiar with the area? _____
2. How many bedrooms do you need? _____
3. What area do you live in now? _____
4. Are you buying or renting at this time? _____
5. When can you see this property? _____

PRICE
6. Is this the price range you're interested in? _____
7. How much do you want to invest in a home? $_____ (down pay)
8. Is your house on the market? _____
   I would like to see it! _____
9. What type of home do you prefer? Rambler ___ Split ___ Colonial ___
10. How many children do you have? ___ What ages? _
11. Schools: Public _____
    Parochial _____
    High School _____
12. When would you want possession of another home?
13. Perhaps you would care to come by our office and go over our listings with me and we could save time in getting a better idea of what you want! Could you make it today? _____
14. Can you see this property today? _____
15. Remarks—Special needs _____
    _____
    _____

Appointment made? Yes ___ No ___ Sale resulted? _____
Date of call _____ 19__ Salesman _____

Courtesy of Booher & Day

Figure 9-3

174

DAILY SCHEDULE

DAY _____ DATE _____ HOURS _____

My Goal for 19___ is _____

Today I will succeed at: _____ A Listing _____ A Sale _____

A Closing _____

Time		Phone Calls to Make
8:00	_____	_____
8:30	_____	_____
9:00	_____	_____
9:30	_____	_____
10:00	_____	_____
10:30	_____	_____
11:00	_____	_____
11:30	_____	_____
12:00	_____	**Priorities**
12:30	_____	_____
1:00	_____	_____
1:30	_____	_____
2:00	_____	_____
2:30	_____	_____
3:00	_____	_____
3:30	_____	_____
4:00	_____	_____
4:30	_____	**Checklist**
5:00	_____	Canvassing _____
5:30	_____	Prospecting _____
6:00	_____	Direct Mail _____
6:30	_____	Floor Duty _____
7:00	_____	Other _____

Figure 9-4

Each day they should write down their goal for today, this month, this year. It will serve as a constant reminder and motivator to accomplish what they have determined is important.

9-10. Competitive Market Analysis

Prepared by the National Association of Realtors, this form is an excellent tool for persuading sellers on fair market value, and should be included in every agent's listing presentation. It also forces your agents to do their homework and be prepared to offer an accurate opinion of value on the property. With this added ammunition, the seller will find it difficult to argue with the agent's professional opinion of the value of his or her home. These forms are available for a reasonable fee from the National Association of Realtors. (See Figure 9-5.)

9-11. Closing Progress Report and Pending File

While this form is basically self-explanatory, you should review it with your agents to ensure they understand the importance of it, and with whom the responsibility lies for each aspect of the transaction. This form allows you, each morning, to quickly review the status of your pending files and follow up on any details requiring your attention. (See Figure 9-6.)

9-12. Monthly Income Record

This form will help you keep a running total of how well your agent is doing, compared with his or her annual goal. You will also be able to tell how he or she is doing compared with previous months. The income listed on this form should be for offers taken and listings that have offers on them during each month, and not for actual commissions received during this 30-day period. What you are gauging is activity and productivity. You are not concerned with actual money paid at this point, since that does not tell you how productive the agent has been this month. (See Figure 9-7.)

Competitive Market Analysis

Property Address _____ Date _____

For Sale Now:	Bed-rms.	Baths	Den	Sq. Ft.	1st Loan	List Price	Days on Market		Terms	

Sold Past 12 Mos.	Bed-rms.	Baths	Den	Sq. Ft.	1st Loan	List Price	Days on Market	Date Sold	Sale Price	Terms

Expired Past 12 Mos.	Bed-rms.	Baths	Den	Sq. Ft.	1st Loan	List	Days on Market		Terms	

F.H.A. Appraisals

Address	Appraisal	Address	Appraisal

Buyer Appeal   **Marketing Position**

(Grade each item 0 to 20 ... basis of desirability or urgency)

Buyer Appeal		Marketing Position	
1 Fine Location	_____ %	1 Why Are They Selling _____	%
2 Exciting Extras	_____ %	2 How Soon Must They Sell _____	%
3 Extra Special Financing	_____	3 Will They Help Finance .... Yes___ No___	%
4 Exceptional Appeal	_____	4 Will They List at Competitive Market Value ... Yes___ No___	%
5 Under Market Price _____ Yes		5 Will They Pay for Appraisal .... Yes___ No___	%

Rating Total _____ %   Rating Total _____ %

Assets _____
Drawbacks _____
Area Market Conditions _____

Recommended Terms _____

Selling

Brokerage	
Loan Payoff	$
Prepayment Privilege	$
FHA — VA Points	$
Title and Escrow Fees: IRS Stamps. Recons. Recording	$
Termite Clearance	$
Misc. Payoffs: 2nd T.D., Pool, Patio, Water Softener, Fence, Improvement Bond.	$
	$
	$
Total	$

Top Competitive Market Value $ _____

Probable Final Sales Price $ _____

Total Selling Costs $ _____

Net Proceeds $ _____   Plus or Minus $ _____

The statements and figures presented herein, while not guaranteed, are secured from sources we believe authoritative.   Prepared by _____

Figure 9-5

PROGRESS REPORT

SELLER _____ PHONE _____ ADDRESS _____

BUYER _____ PHONE _____ ADDRESS _____

ADDRESS OF PROPERTY _____ DATE OF OFFER _____ ACCEPTED _____

SELLING PRICE _____ SALESMAN _____ LISTING AGENT _____

DATE EARNEST MONEY DEPOSITED _____ AMOUNT _____ ABSTRACT AT _____

FINANCING REQUIRED   CONV   VA   MAGIC   CONTRACT   PLEDGE OTHER _____

PRESENT MORTAGE HELD BY _____ ESCROW AGENT (IF CONTRACT) _____

COPY OF OTP TO _____ DATE _____ TO _____ DATE _____

DATE OF LOAN APPLICATION _____ WITH _____

DATE CREDIT REPORT ORDERED _____ BUYER POINTS _____ SELLER POINTS _____

DOES SELLER AGREE TO PAY ANYMORE THAN HIS NORMAL COSTS?   (YES)   (NO)   IF YES _____

PLEASE ELABORATE _____

APPRAISAL FEE ADVANCED BY _____ TERMITE INSP. _____ DATE _____

DATE MAILED FOR APPROVAL (MGIC FHA VA) _____ LOAN APPROVED _____

ABSTRACT PICKED UP AT _____ DATE _____

ABSTRACT DELIVERED TO _____ DATE _____

ABSTRACT DELIVERED TO _____ DATE _____

ABSTRACT DELIVERED TO _____ DATE _____

CONTRACT PREPARATION BY _____ DEED PREPARED BY _____

IF CONTRACT   DATE CONTRACTS, DEED, ABSTRACT, PICKED UP _____

IF CONTRACT   PICK UP ESCROW FORMS FROM ESCROW AGENT _____ DATE _____

CLOSING TIME SET FOR _____ DATE _____ PLACE _____

SELLERS NOTIFIED _____ ADVISED ON INSURANCE _____

BUYERS NOTIFIED _____

ANY PAPERS OUR OFFICE NEEDS RETURNED TO LENDER OR ESCROW AGENT _____ DATE _____

THIS TRANSACTION WAS CLOSED AT _____ DATE _____

KEY RETURNED TO _____ CLOSING BROKER _____

SALESMAN RESPONSIBLE FOR SOLD SIGN _____ DATE _____

REMARKS:

Figure 9-6

MONTHLY INCOME RECORD

_____ 1976

SALES	JAN	FEB	MARCH	APRIL	MAY	JUNE	JULY	AUG	SEPT	OCT	NOV	DEC
Listings Sold												
Listings Taken												
Listings Expired												
Sales Commission												
Listing Commission												
Total												

YEAR TO DATE

SALES	JAN	FEB	MARCH	APRIL	MAY	JUNE	JULY	AUG	SEPT	OCT	NOV	DEC
Listings Sold												
Listing Taken												
Listings Expired												
Sales Commission												
Listing Commission												
Total												

Figure 9-7

9-13. Daily Worksheet Report

This is the real indicator of how productively your agent is utilizing his or her time. This form breaks the agent's activities down into several categories for each day of the month. A quick review of this form will tell you if the agent has been doing the right things to produce business. Also, by comparing a poor month with a good month, you can point out to your agent the difference in activities when he or she was generating several sales or listings. When the agent sees in black and white that during a poor month he or she made fewer calls, didn't canvass, didn't check out the "Hot 100" list, etc., it will be obvious to him or her why this month wasn't productive. (See Figure 9-8.)

9-14. Prospect Data Card

Available through New England Business Services, the Prospect Data Card provides your agents with all of the information they need on a prospect at one quick glance. These cards should always be near the agent, so he can match them with new listings or make calls when generating new business. Too many potential clients are lost simply because the salesperson doesn't keep track of the prospect's name, address, and housing needs. (See Figure 9-9.)

9-15. Detailed Listing Card

Also available from New England Business Services, the Detailed Listing Card gives your agents a handy, detailed profile of your listings, and makes it easier to come up with information on a property while they are discussing it with a prospect. The reverse side of the card provides a log for the agent to use in keeping a record of clients who were shown the property and their responses. (See Figure 9-10.)

9-16. Advertising Analysis

Advertising costs represent the largest expenditure in the operation of a real estate business. To succeed at the highest profit margin possible, you must know where your advertising dollars are going, which advertising is the most effective, and which advertising does not return the dollars invested.

To ensure that you are making the best use of your advertising dollar and reaching the goals you have set for your advertising program, it is imperative that you monitor your advertising results closely. The following form provides you the format to determine the effectiveness of each ad or other method of advertising. (See Figure 9-11.)

9-17. Closing Record, Year-to-Date

This form is easy to complete, provides you with a quick, accurate indication of the status of your office compared with your goal, and enables you to compile several pieces of useful information in one report.

Each day you will not only know the number of closings, year-to-date, but you will also have at your fingertips the property addresses, names of buyers and sellers, type of financing used, salesperson and listing agent involved, and year-to-date earnings for the office and each salesperson associated with your firm. (See Figure 9-12.)

9-18. Salespeoples' Commission Record

This form is designed in the same style and format as the Closing Record, Year-to-Date, except that it is for the use of each individual salesperson. It serves as a record for the salespeople of the number of closings they have had, and is also an excellent record for tax purposes.

More importantly, though, your salespeople should use this record when evaluating their activity. It provides them with the sales price of the property, type of financing, whether their commission was for a listing or a sale, and the location of the property. From these records they will know in which price range they are the most successful, which type of financing they seem to use the most often and, in turn, the type of buyer they work with the most often, the number of transactions in which they were involved, and the average commission they earned in the previous year.

By using this information properly, your salespeople will know their strengths and their weaknesses, how to increase their

Whalen Real Estate

Salesman _____

DAILY WORKSHEET REPORT

	Office Calls on Ads	Sign's Phone Calls	Drop-In Clients	No. of Homes Shown	Calls to Past Buyers	Calls for New Listings	New Listings Obtained	Sales Made	OBO Prop's Shown	Calls to Active Clients	Open Home Clients	REMARKS
Mon.												
Tues.												
Wed.												
Thurs.												
Fri.												
Sat.												
Sun.												
Weekly Total												
Mon.												
Tues.												
Wed.												
Thurs.												

Week Ending

			Week Ending						
Fri.									
Sat.									
Sun.									
Weekly Total									
Mon.									
Tues.									
Wed.									
Thurs.									
Fri.									
Sat.									
Sun.									
Weekly Total		Week Ending							
Mon.									
Tues.									
Wed.									
Thurs.									
Fri.									
Sat.									
Sun.									
Weekly Total		Week Ending							
4 WEEKS TOTAL									

Figure 9-8

PROSPECT DATA CARD	NAME		☐ BUY ☐ RENT				PROSPECT DATA CARD
	ADDRESS		DATE				
			HOME PHONE				
	BUS. ADDRESS		BUS. PHONE				
	NO. OF CHILDREN	AGES OF GIRLS		AGES OF BOYS			
	CASH DOWN	PRICE RANGE	MONTHLY PAYMENTS	GI	FHA	CONV.	
	TYPE OF HOUSE DESIRED		ROOMS NEEDED	BATHS NEEDED	BEDROOMS NEEDED		
	SPECIAL REQUIREMENTS (LOCATION DESIRED. ETC.)						
	PRESENT HOME ☐ OWN? ☐ RENT?	INCOME	OCCUPATION				
	HEARD OF US FROM		SALESMAN				

FORM -146 Available from /NEBS/ Inc., Groton. Mass. 01450

Figure 9-9

Product 146, Available from NEBS, Inc., 500 Main St., Groton, MA 01471.

DETAIL LISTING CARD	ADDRESS		LOT SIZE	ROOMS	PRICE	DETAIL LISTING CARD
	LOCATION		BEDROOMS	TYPE		
	OWNER	ADDRESS		PHONE		
	AGE	GAS	FIREPLACE			
	CONDITION	WATER	SCREENS			
	CONSTRUCTION	HOT WATER	S. WINDOWS			
	GARAGE	PLUMBING	LAUNDRY			
	PORCH-B' WAY	SEWERAGE	HATCHWAY			
	ROOF	ELECTRICITY	DRIVEWAY			
	INSULATION	CLOSETS	SIDEWALK			
	HEAT-FUEL	BATHS	STREET			
	1ST FLOOR		TYPE FLOORS			
	2ND FLOOR		TYPE FLOORS			
	3RD FLOOR		TYPE FLOORS			
	CELLAR		HEATING COST			
	ASSESSMENT	TAXES	MORTGAGE	RATE	PAYMENT	BANK
	SCHOOLS		POSSIBLE RENT	KEYS AT		
	DATE AVAILABLE	LISTED BY		DATE		

(OVER)

Figure 9-10

Product 148, Available from NEBS, Inc., 500 Main St., Groton, MA 01471.

ADVERTISING ANALYSIS

MONTH _____   OFFICE _____

LISTINGS TAKEN _____   OFFERS RECEIVED _____

CLOSINGS _____   GROSS INCOME _____

TELEPHONE CALLS ON PROPERTIES _____ TO LIST _____

WALK-INS ON PROPERTIES _____ TO LIST _____

CALLS OR WALK-INS ON: SIGNS _____ LINE ADS _____ PICTURE ADS __

OTHER _____ EXPLAIN _____

CALLS ON # 1. _____   2. _____   3. _____   4. _____   5. _____

6. _____   7. _____   8. _____   9. _____   10. _____   11. _____

12. _____   13. _____   14. _____   15. _____   16. _____   17. _____

18. _____   19. _____   20. _____   21. _____   22. _____   23. _____

24. _____   25. _____   26. _____   27. _____   28. _____   29. _____

30. _____   31. _____   32. _____   33. _____   34. _____   35. _____

36. _____   37. _____   38. _____   39. _____   40. _____   41. _____

42. _____   43. _____   44. _____   45. _____   46. _____   47. _____

48. _____   49. _____   50. _____   51. _____   52. _____   53. _____

54. _____   55. _____   56. _____   57. _____   58. _____   59. _____

60. _____   61. _____   62. _____   63. _____   64. _____   65. _____

Gross Income _____   Advertising $ Divided by Gross Income =

Advertising $ _____   % of Income Spent on Advertising.

(Always number each property within each ad so you can evaluate which copy was the most effective. Keep a scrapbook of all advertising for comparison.)

Figure 9-11

income, and if they are working with the type of buyers and sellers who are most likely to make them as successful as they want to be. (See Figure 9-13.)

9-19. Goal Form

Your expertise will be needed here more than with any other form. The salesperson will not know if he or she is being too conservative or too optimistic. Until the agent has been selling for a

SANDIFAR-MISNER ASSOCIATES CLOSING RECORD

No.	Property Address	Date Closed	Buyer	Seller	Sales Price	Comm.	Type of Fin.	Over Ride	Office Comm.	Listing Agent	Selling Agent
1	114 Locust Lane	1/4	Isaac	Gray	42,500	2975.	M.G.I.C.	25.	1105.	Jim S.	Andrew A.
2	8115 Walnut Dr.	1/4	Mays	Nelson	56,000	3920.	Cash	25.	1543.	Nancy J.	Nancy J.
3	2112 S. 18th St.	1/5	Wise	Mays	72,000	5040.	Conventional	25.	1991.	Edward H.	John S.
4	Trailways Campgd.	1/5	Adams	Johnson	115,000	8050.	Wrap-a-round	25.	3195.	Lois J.	Jim S.
5	R.R. 1 Box 19N	1/5	Rick	Crompton	62,000	4340.	Conventional	25.	1711.	Edward H.	Lois J.
6	Fuller Farm	1/5	Jones	Asher	256,000	17920.	Contract	25.	7143.	Andrew A.	Andrew A.
7	313 W.Main	1/6	Cox	Wilson	31,000	2170.	V.A.	25.	843.	John S.	Jim S.

CLOSING RECORD—PART 2

NO.	JIM SIMPSON	NANCY JAMES	ANDREW ARTHUR	LOIS JOHNSON	JOHN SIMON	EDWARD HINES
1	892.50		892.50			
2		2352.00				
3					1512.00	1512.00
4	2415.00			2415.00		
5				1302.00		1302.00
6			10,752.00			
7	651.00				651.00	

Figure 9-13

186

COMMISSION RECORD FOR YEAR-TO-DATE						
ADDRESS	BUYER	SELLER	DATE	FIN.	S-L	COMM.

Figure 9-13

while, he or she can't know what to expect in the way of commissions or earnings. The new agent is also likely to know very little about planning for a $30,000 income.

You will have to tell the agent how many calls he or she must make, how many showings and presentations are necessary, and on which activities the most time should be spent to reap the most reward.

With your aid, this form will be more than a motivator. It will actually tell the agent what must be done every day, every week, every month, to reach the income level he or she desires. If the agent follows the formula and does those things listed, he or she will succeed.

As a sales manager, you must provide guidance without subduing the agent's enthusiasm by being conservative in your estimation of his or her earning potential, and without giving a goal so high that the agent will become disillusioned about being able to reach it. Another problem with goals is reaching them too soon. In my first year in real estate sales, I reached my goal in November. I had no incentive to continue being aggressive or hungry. I wanted to sit back and pat myself on the back for a job well done. If you have a salesperson who is obviously going to exceed his or her goal because of having a great year, catch it as early as possible and motivate this person to raise that goal and direct all efforts to the *super goal.* Keep the agent reaching for a new high, proud of what has been accomplished, but determined to see what heights he or she can attain. (See Figure 9-14.)

GOAL FOR _____

MY GOAL FOR 19__ is $_____

To reach my goal I need to make $_____ each month.

In order to make $_____ per month, I will sell _____ homes and have _____ listings sell each month.

I will make the following calls to obtain my goal:

    A. I expect to spend _____ hours per week actively working my real estate business.

    B. I will show _____ prospects each month.

    C. I will ask _____ prospects to look at property each month.

    D. I will make _____ calls for/on prospects each month.

    E. I will ask _____ owners to list each month.

    F. I will give my listing presentation to _____ prospects each month.

    G. I will list _____ properties each month.

    H. I will hold _____ open houses during the year.

Sales Manager
Sandifar-Misner Associates

Salesperson

Date

Figure 9-14

9-20. *Listing Evaluation Form*

Each salesperson should have a supply of these with him during the tour of homes each week. After inspecting the property, each salesperson fills out the form and gives it to the listing agent. The listing agent can then compile them and determine the average appraised value of the property and any conditions that the consensus shows needs to be corrected. He or she should then report to the owner of the property the results. Used properly, these forms will help convince the owner if the listing is too high, or if repairs need to be made. They can also help motivate your salespeople if the combined appraisal is higher than the listed price. (See Figure 9-15.)

9-21. *Utilizing the Fullest Potential Your Forms Provide*

While the forms I have given you offer many advantages and help you meet several goals, the benefit you will derive comes down to what you are really after: *They Will Help You and Your Salespeople*

```
┌─────────────────────────────────────────────────────────┐
│                  LISTING EVALUATION                       │
│  PROPERTY ADDRESS _____     │
│  SELLER _____     │
│  LISTING AGENT _____     │
│  ESTIMATE OF VALUE_____      │
│  CONDITIONS NEEDING ATTENTION _____      │
│  _____       │
│  _____       │
│  COMMENTS _____      │
│  _____       │
│  _____       │
│  _____       │
│  _____       │
│  _____      _____             │
│  DATE                  SALESPERSON                        │
└─────────────────────────────────────────────────────────┘
```

Figure 9-15

Make More Money! Everything you do in business boils down to your ultimate goal of increasing your earnings. If it doesn't, don't do it.

You can and will realize that goal by implementing the fifteen forms in this chapter. Each is designed to improve communication, bring out weaknesses so they can be corrected, keep records for follow-up, and make it easier for a salesperson to put together a transaction and earn a commission. To achieve this end, however, the user must keep in mind the purpose of each form. If they become habit, if they are taken for granted, if they are completed less than honestly or haphazardly, and if the advice they offer is not received, they are a waste of valuable selling time. Only through consistent, precise, and objective use can the full potential of these forms be recognized.

10

Successful Techniques
For Motivating
Real Estate Salespeople

Working with various sized real estate offices and in different regions across the United States, I find that many of the problems and frustrations faced by sales managers are the same, regardless of size, experience, number of salespeople, or area of the country. Even with part-time versus full-time salespeople, the problems are similar; only the solutions are different. Motivating salespeople is one of the problems faced by all sales managers and one that causes more failures than training, economy, or ability. Motivation can also cause success, and Chapter Ten will reveal how other sales managers have used motivation to make their agents and their office successful, even in tight money markets or low turnover areas.

10-1. *Motivating the Motivator*

Before you can motivate anyone else, you must first be motivated yourself. Nothing comes through as obviously as a motivator who does not believe in his or her people or techniques. Entertainers, nurses, doctors, politicians, and athletes are examples of people who must transmit positive attitudes regardless of circumstances. Sales managers must also remain optimistic, positive, excited, and committed to the individual, if they are to motivate those under them. Your personality and style then become the all-important motivating tools.

Don't underestimate your own need for motivational support. Constantly being involved with agents who are down, attentive to the problems of the brokerage, and concerned with your own personal problems provides you with daily opportunities to lose your own motivation and your ability to motivate others. To protect yourself against these drains on your positive attitude, develop a daily program of self-motivation.

The following tips will enable you to maintain a high level of motivation:

1. Keep your aspiration level high by dreaming of goals you want to accomplish.
2. Let others motivate you. Spend time with those who are positive thinkers and successful in their professions.
3. Use motivational tapes while driving to and from the office and appointments.
4. Regularly redefine your goals so you do not lose the motivational effect they provide you.
5. Think success. Momentary set-backs do not mean you are unsuccessful. Regardless of how successful a person is, his or her entire career is littered with obstacles. Winners overcome these hurdles and are strengthened from them. Even the failure of a project does not affect the overall success of your career.

10-2. The Power of Motivation

Motivating a salesperson without training them will only make them temporarily successful, but training salespeople without motivating them will not bring about any success. Many of us fail to realize just how much of an effect the right motivation can have on the success of our salespeople.

I first realized the amazing power of motivation when I was seventeen years old. I had answered an ad for an appliance salesmen and found myself sitting among fifteen other young men applying for the position. The sales manager brought out the company's product and gave us a demonstration of the many and varied functions the machine was capable of performing. He then discussed how, with each sale, our commissions were increased and how much money could be made selling this marvelous new product. At the conclusion of his presentation, he made an unusual offer. We had a choice between working on salary or commission. He would pay us a straight salary of $150. per week (Not bad money back then) or on the accelerated commission schedule.

Out of the sixteen of us sitting there, not one chose the straight salary. In the first week I made $400, and it was almost two weeks before I realized I was selling vacuum cleaners. That man had so well convinced a seventeen-year-old boy that he could sell vacuum cleaners disguised as appliances that he actually went out and did it.

After a few weeks, I was asked to go to the distribution center and pick up a supply of vacuum cleaners. Signing the ticket for them, I realized this man was paying $50.00 for a product I was selling for $300.00. A few days later, one of the girls that called prospects and made the appointments for us was absent, so the sales manager ask me to make some calls. As a door opener, we offered a book of trading stamps to the prospect for listening to our presentation. After a day on the telephone, I discovered that the prospects were only interested in getting their trading stamps, where before I was led to believe that they were inviting us into their home.

Within a week, I couldn't have given one of those vacuum cleaners away. Nothing had changed, except my knowledge of the system and my mental attitude. The product was the same, the prospects were the same, only now I was no longer positive or aggressive. Without realizing it, my sales manager had stopped motivating me, and had subjected me to the negative aspects of the selling process.

Sales managers can learn a lesson from the experience of a seventeen-year-old. You can never stop motivating your salespeople. You have to act as a shield from the negative aspects of our business and make the agents concentrate on the positive. You have the opportunity to take a salesperson to greater heights than he or she ever imagined possible, further than possible without you. You also have opportunities to subject your agents to negative motivation. Consider which you are doing when you implement new policies, hold a sales meeting, or broadcast the status of the office to your salespeople. Each day, find a means of motivating your agents in a positive manner. Over the short run, motivation will cause success. Add this to your training efforts and you can sustain a successful career for your salespeople.

10-3. *Motivating with Incentives*

Each person reacts to his or her own form of motivation. While many sales managers attempt to use money or prizes as incentives, the results are usually discouraging. The reason for such little success in motivating with incentives is that, if a person won't work hard for a $1,000 commission, adding 5 percent to it or offering a trip won't motivate him or her to work any harder.

There are times, however, when financial or prize incentives can be very effective. If you have successful agents who are close to their goal or are "money-hungry," these incentives will cause them to put in that extra hour, or ask for a sale that second time. In most cases, however, it is not the reward or additional earnings that motivate salespeople to work harder. It is the competition that goes along with the reward. The honor of being the best or beating out their associates will get many people moving who would otherwise not make that extra effort.

If you have structured your commission schedule so that the percent of the agent's commission increases with his or her annual volume of sales, you've probably already discovered that only those who were going to reach the higher plateau anyway do so. If you've run a listing contest where the only incentive was a cash payment when a listing was secured, you know that the only people increasing their listings were those who were already good listeners.

The problem with this type of motivator is it pits an agent against him- or herself, which is how the agent works everyday. If the agent won't go out and make a sale or get a listing for the base commission, adding to it won't effect the person's production. Competition with other agents, however, will make your salespeople go that extra mile. Not only do they want to win for the sake of beating the others, they also become motivated by the enthusiasm of the other agents.

There are two types of contests that work well with real estate salespeople. The first is an individual contest with each salesperson competing with all other salespeople for the most listings, sales, or appointments within a given time frame. The second involves dividing your staff into two or three groups and awarding a prize to

the entire winning team. The bigger the prize, the more enthusiasm you can generate, but even dinners, gas, or privileges can
be effective, since the real incentive is to beat the other salespeople.

10-4. Using Goals as a Motivator

The use of goals is an excellent method of motivation if the
goals are realistic and reviewed often enough to keep them in the
forefront of the agent's mind. Too many agents prepare their goal
at the first of the year and then put it away, never to be looked at
again. A goal can only be a motivator as long as it is important to the
agent. The secret for the sales manager is to keep that goal very
important and very much in the mind of the individual.

This responsibility can be accomplished in a variety of ways, all
of which should be employed by the sales manager. Following is a
list of opportunities for you to utilize the motivational potential of
an agent's goal.

1. Each month discuss the agent's goal and his or her progress
   toward's reaching it during the personal sales meeting.
2. Encourage your agents to share their goal with their family
   and friends. If others close to the agent are aware of his or
   her amibition, the agent is more likely to work harder to
   reach it.
3. Break the agent's goal down into daily calls. Once the agent
   sees how easy it is to reach this goal, he or she will have
   more enthusiasm for making the calls required each day.
   Follow up and make sure he or she is, in fact, making the
   calls that were determined necessary to earn the income
   desired.
4. Inform your agents that you use their goals to establish
   your budget for the year. The amount you have to allot to
   advertising, office expenses, etc., is predicated on what the
   salespeople plan on earning during the year. If they do not
   reach their goals, your office will fall short of the funds
   necessary to provide the agents with the exposure and sales
   assistance they want and need.
5. Find opportunities to reward or brag about those agents
   that reach their goal each month. Let the other agents
   know achievers are recognized.

Of course, a goal that is too difficult or too easy to reach is not a motivator. Agents who reach their goals early because of hard work and improved techniques also face a letdown during the last few months because they have nothing to drive them and have succeeded at the one accomplishment they were determined to achieve from the first of the year. You have the ability to overcome these problems and keep your agents' goals as their most effective motivating factor. Don't leave the setting and maintaining of goals solely to your agents. You are needed to make their goals work for them.

10-5. *Motivating Real Esate Salespeople with Competition*

As we discussed earlier, incentives will only be successful motivators when combined with competition for them. Competition can also be used in many other ways to motivate your associates.

During my visits to various real estate offices, I have seen sales managers use many creative techniques to motivate through competition. Following are the most successful of these tactics.

1. The Offer Book—The offer book presents two competitive motivators. First, agents feel good about putting their name in the book for the others to see, and will work hard to see their names in the offer book more times each month than anyone else's. Second, when an offer is received on a property, and before it is presented, salespeople will begin to scramble to find a prospect or make one last effort to get a present prospect to make an offer on the home.

2. Tour of Homes—The tour of homes can also be a motivator in two different ways. One listing agent gave the agents a five-minute presentation on the home they had just entered, treating the salespeople as though they were buyers. After pointing out the features of the home, he informed the agents that they had two weeks to sell the property or he would sell it. Asking one of his associates about his seemingly unusual style, I was informed that after the agent had succeeded at his boast a few times, the agents were now believers. The entire office worked

harder on his listings than on anyone else's, because they knew if they didn't find a buyer in a short time, the listing agent would sell the home. If they were to have a chance at earning a commission on his listings, they couldn't mess around.

The tour of homes had a different effect on another agent. After viewing a very attractive home—in fact the nicest listing of the tour—I complimented him on it. "After sitting through the last three sales meetings without a listing, I couldn't take one more week without having a listing to offer. This is *my* home," he advised. Now that's competitive motivation!

3. One Illinois broker takes his entire sales staff to breakfast every morning they tour homes. He only pays for those who have a listing to view, however. "Believe me, no one wants to be the only agent paying for his own breakfast," he commented. "It's not the money—it's the failure he has to admit to when he reaches into his pocket."

4. Office Status—A California sales manager uses his competition in the community to keep his agents hustling. Each week at the sales meeting, he marks a chart indicating the office's gain or loss on their nearest competitor, in both the number of listings and number of sales. By giving his team an outside source to compete against, and in a way his agents can see their efforts pay off, he is able to keep them motivated towards a common goal. Each time a competing office is surpassed, he holds a celebration for his entire staff.

Experiment with different types of competition within your office. Find those motivators that succeed with a majority of your salespeople and, most importantly, keep some form of (friendly) competition alive within your office at all times.

10-6. Using the Motivation Tools Available to You

More than likely you have more motivational tools available to you than you are presently using. First let's take a look at those in-house tools you can begin utilizing immediately.

10-6A. *Survival*

Certainly one means of motivation is to put groceries on the table. When I first entered the real estate business, it seemed that every time I was introduced to an agent from another office, they commented on the amazing success I had enjoyed so early in my career. They probably wouldn't have been nearly so impressed if they had realized it was not due to my abilities, but rather to the fact that I was broke when I began selling and the rent was due. I succeeded because I worked over 90 hours a week. And I worked over 90 hours a week because I had to sell quickly or starve.

10-6B. *Competition*

The majority of salespeople will work harder to prove themselves to their peers, to win, than they will to put more dollars into their own pockets. Keep the competition friendly, direct the competition so you can control it, and maintain it on a constant basis.

10-6C. *Recognition*

People leave organizations because they feel they are not appreciated or recognized for their accomplishments. Awards, pictures in the paper, public recognition, recognition at sales meetings, plaques, and personal praise should all be used to bolster the ego of the individual agent. Find ways to recognize those agents who put in the effort, regardless of their success. The key is to keep them making the effort, since experience proves that success is assured by the number of calls made and effort exerted.

10-6D. *Confidence*

New salespeople, in particular, have difficulty believing in themselves. Anyone has to believe they can do something before they can. Bolster the confidence of your salespeople by tearing away their fears and recognizing their successes. I was recently involved in a discussion with a new agent who was very insecure about what he had to offer prospects. "You can tell buyers and sellers that you are the best because you have the experience and track record behind you to back up your claims. I can't go out and tell people they should list their home with me rather than you because I can provide them better service, because I can't. I simply can't compete with you or most of the other experienced agents I have to in order to get a listing or a buying prospect."

I realized this agent was never going to succeed until he had the confidence that he could compete with other agents, and that he could provide the best service in town for his clients. To help him overcome this feeling, I ask him to consider what he just said. Did I care more about a client than he did? Did I have more technical knowledge about housing construction, financing, or the market than he? Would I work harder and protect my client's interest more than he? No, of course not! Those are the factors that clients are concerned about. Yes, I was a better *salesman* than he was, because I had more experience and I knew how to handle buyers and sellers; but clients don't hire me for salesmenship, they hire me to help them. His personal service is what made him the best agent in town—at least to that particular client—because no one was going to be more concerned about the needs of that client than he.

10-6E. Training

Training is one of the greatest motivators you can use, because not only does it bolster the confidence of the agent, but also, salespeople are also anxious to get out into the field and try the new techniques you have given them. Since training in itself will motivate your salespeople, your training program should be a continuous operation, regardless of the amount of experience of your salespeople.

Besides these five in-house motivators available to you, you should utilize as many outside motivational programs as possible. Tapes that your agents can take home with them, listen to in the car, or play while on floor duty will keep them "pumped up" on a daily basis. Seminars and lectures should also be attended on a regular basis for the sole purpose of inspiring your agents, even for a short period of time.

10-7. *Recognizing and Meeting Individual Needs for Motivation*

One of the things that makes motivating a sales staff in a real estate office so difficult is that our salespeople come from all walks of life and sell real estate for a variety of reasons. We employ a mixture of housewives, retirees, young agents, middle-aged salespeople and older ones. Their experience varies as much as their reasons for being in the real estate profession. Each of these individuals requires a different type of motivation and a different approach, based on their personality and motive for being in the real estate business. Some will react to one of the motivational techniques we have discussed, while others may respond to many or all of the incentives you place before them.

As sales managers, we often feel we cannot motivate those salespeople who do not have a financial need or are not ego driven. The fact is that everyone has a motivational "hot spot" we can trigger if we are observant enough to locate it. Just because a salesperson doesn't respond to the same motivation as the rest of the staff, it doesn't mean they cannot be motivated. A woman whose career merely provides a supplement to her husband's income may be motivated enough to devote extra hours to her real estate business if you implant the dream of taking her family on a vacation to Hawaii or her husband on a cruise. A retiree may be motivated by your seeking his or her help in developing the talents of the younger agents in your office by putting his or her experience in other fields to use to better train your less experienced staff. A long-time agent who has not reached the level of success you know is possible may be motivated by pointing out the things he or she could have, but does not.

Some agents respond to fear, competition, survival, ego, money, success, recognition, achievement, or even self-satisfaction. An agent who is not motivated, however, hasn't had the right push on his "hot spot." Your job is to uncover which of these motivations will unleash the drive needed by the agent to succeed. History has shown that no particular personality type, physical attribute, motivation, or experience dictates success in our industry. Many of the most successful salespeople in the world are those you would least suspect of having the qualities necessary to succeed. Something all successful people have in common is a reason to be successful. A sales manager, a family member, a friend, or a teacher at some point triggered the one key within those individuals that made them want, and even need, to excel. Your salespeople, even your lowest producers, also have that hidden need within them. Take the time to discover it, and both of you will be rewarded.

10-8. How Motivational Techniques Have Been Used Successfully by Others

Maybe I can best explain what the right type of motivation can do for your sales staff and how you can develop successful motivational techniques by examples of what powerful, effective motivation has accomplished for others.

John H. had been selling real estate for six months and had only made one sale. He had a couple of listings, but they were overpriced and in a slow turnover neighborhood. His sales manager, Jim P., was stumped for a solution to get John moving. He had a good personality, was educated, and certainly had a financial need to succeed, but all of Jim's efforts up to this point had failed.

Thinking about John one day, Jim remembered that John was an athlete in high school and college. Rather than concentrate on personal motivation for John, Jim decided to work on John's competitive nature as a means of motivating him.

First, Jim designed a listing contest that ran for two weeks. After dividing the sales staff into two groups, Jim assigned John as captain of his team. Making John the leader for his group was the key to Jim's plan. John now felt he had to pull his share, put in that extra effort to win, not just for himself, but for his team as well. In two weeks, John listed six properties and received four buying prospects from this group. Not only did his team win, but once John experienced success, he worked harder and with more confidence than any other agent in the office. By the end of his first year, even with a slow first six months, John had earned over $32,000 in commissions.

The old adage, "Success Breeds Success" is very true. Once you have been able to give a salesperson a taste of success, that experience will become a motivating force for him or her.

A recession hits a record-producing plant particularly hard, since the first item people give up when money is tight is their records. During one of these periods, one record company had been down in orders for over 13 months. With over 60 percent of their work force laid off, most employees were lucky to work three or four days a month. In the record business, an order must be pressed and shipped very quickly, since favorite recordings do not stay at the top of the charts for a very long period of time. This also means that employees know that when an order is completed, they will be out of work. It is one of the few industries I know of where, if the company is to succeed, the employees must literally work themselves out of a job.

Having been hired to do some consulting work for them, I began to notice that new production records were being set each day. This was extremely surprising to me since, for several weeks, the plant had been on a three- and four-day work week. Why would people work this hard, produce this much, knowing that by doing so, they would not have enough work to last them for the entire week?

To uncover the answer, I looked up the press room supervisor and ask him for his secret. "At the end of first shift, I write the day's production on the chalkboard. When the second shift comes on and sees the production level reached by the first shift, they set their goal at beating that figure. When the first shift comes back on, they look to see if the second beat their production the night before. They then work hard to keep the level high enough so that the second shift can't beat them. It's the pride of the individual worker and the shift as a team that makes them strive to be the best."

If a supervisor can get his people to work themselves out of a full week's pay check with competition, surely you can get your salespeople to work themselves into bigger paychecks using the same technique.

Ed was 47 years old. He had been selling real estate for 10 years and was well respected in the community. Before Ed entered the real estate field, he worked in a factory, earning the same amount of money year after year. When the factory closed, he got his real estate license and, since the job market was slow, began selling real estate. Ed decided when he went into real estate that he needed to make $12,000 a year. Regardless of the economic cycle during those ten years, Ed made $12,000. As housing prices began to rise twenty, thirty, forty percent, Ed still made $12,000. That was the amount of money he was used to making and what he needed to maintain his family in the style to which they had been accustomed.

New salespeople would come to the office and quickly surpass Ed's earnings, while others would join the sales staff and soon drop out of real estate sales because they couldn't make a living. Ed still earned his $12,000, seemingly unaffected by the successes or failures of the others.

When a new sales manager was hired, one of his first tasks was to review the sales history of each agent and consider what he could do to help the agents increase their income. He was amazed at Ed's earnings record, but immediately realized the problem. Anyone good enough to maintain an income level he had determined to be his goal had the ability to sell, but was limiting his earnings to the amount he conceived as his required income.

The sales manager called Ed into the office and discussed his sales record. Ed was pleased with himself for achieving his goal each year and maintaining a steady income level year after year.

"Ed, do you realize that rather than succeeding, you are actually depriving yourself and your family of the many advantages and income three or four times what you have been earning could provide? *You* are limiting your income by being satisfied with what you need, rather than by using what you would like to have as your goal. Your past steadiness proves you have the ability to sell real estate and earn any amount you want to earn. This month, rather than using the $1,000 goal that you need to live on as a guideline, I want you to think of something your family would really like to have: a mink coat for your wife, a family vacation to a nice resort, a car for your son, or perhaps a new boat. But think of something you would like to have, not something you have to have. Think about the excitement of your family when you spring your surprise on them. Image yourself and your family enjoying that vacation. Then I want you to go home and tell your family about your plans and make a commitment to making them come true.

"Do this for me for just one month. You deserve it and your family deserves it. Take off the straightjacket you have placed on yourself, and spend one month in pursuit of a dream."

Ed did as his sales manager asked, and with his wife and son, decided on a three-week vacation to the west, first class. They would stay in the finest hotels, see all of the attractions, and take all the time they needed. Ed worked with new commitment. He seemed to be running as he called on new prospects. At the end of the month, he had sold four homes, listed three properties and one of them had sold. For the first time in his real estate selling career, Ed earned over $4,000 in one month.

Once again, the sales manager called Ed into his office. "Ed, I'm proud of you for reaching your goal, but I'm not surprised. You can have earnings as good or better than this every month, because you know how to sell real estate. You were the one who decided you would earn $12,000 a year, not the buyers or the sellers. Now that you have proven to yourself that you are worth $50,000 a year, let's sit down and establish a new goal for this year."

Ed never again earned less than $40,000 a year. Once he had removed the barricades in his own mind, he was ready to enjoy the success he was capable of earning.

11

"52" Sales Meetings That Train, Motivate And Communicate

The value of a strong sales meeting is obvious just by comparing the success of offices having creative, effective sales meetings with those that continually offer the same lack-luster effort each week. The pace and atmosphere set at these sesssions, as well as the training possibilities, can greatly determine the success of your salespeople.

Knowing that a high-geared and informative sales meeting can mean more success for your office, and finding the time and expertise to put together 52 such sessions each year are two different things. With the time-consuming duties involved with closings, advertising, selling, and training, it is easy to neglect your preparation and planning that must go into a successful sales meeting. Chapter Eleven will alleviate these problems by providing you with 52 ideas and formats for using your sales meetings to motivate, communicate and train your salespeople.

11-1. What Your Sales Meetings Should Do—for You and Your Salespeople

Being a sales manager, you know the importance of setting goals, of pre-planning where you want to be, or the desired result of your endeavors. The same thing can be said for your sales meetings. They should be a means of fulfilling your overall goal for your office. These sessions should be designed to take your salespeople, step-by-step, to where you want them to be. When you are consulting with salespeople in individual sessions, you work towards overcoming their individual problems and reaching their goals by strengthening their weaknesses. You realize when doing this that each person is an individual and, therefore, requires different types of advice. While your goal is basically the same with your weekly group sales meetings, the methods you use must be different. You have to reach your entire sales force with the same presentation, and generate the same commitment from each of them. The result will be that your salespeople begin to take on an identity as a group and begin to adopt the same goals and attitudes. This is not to say that you want all of your salespeople to think alike or perform in the same manner. Individuality and creativity are important keys to a successful salesperson and a successful office. But you *do* want your agents to have the same aggressive attitude, to live by the same rules, and to have the same degree of expertise in all areas of selling.

The best vehicle available for reaching this goal is your sales meeting. You can communicate new facts about listings, new policies, and new methods. You can motivate your entire sales force to get them behind new programs, to generate activity in new areas, and to propel them to more sales and increased listings. You can also use your weekly sessions for training since everyone, new or experienced, constantly needs additional training in all phases of selling.

Salespeople need three things to be successful over a long period of time: knowledge, desire, and a good sales manager. If you fit the bill on the third requirement, you will provide them with the other two.

Each sales meeting you conduct should do three things:

1. Communicate
2. Motivate
3. Train

Meeting these three criteria is not only good business for you, but also your duty towards your salespeople. You, as their manager, have an obligation to provide your agents with every tool available to increase their earnings. They associate with your office because they feel you can enable them to make a better living than any other office in your community. When you can't, they will begin to look for greener pastures, and rightfully so. Regardless of any loyalty you might feel they owe you, they have a greater obligation to give themselves and their families the best living they possibly can. The surest way to retain your agents is to be sure that they cannot make a better living anywhere else. If your sales meetings are effective, they will be a source of motivation and training that will provide your agents with the tools they need to increase their income. These agents will remain with your office because, without the guidance they receive in these meetings, they won't be able to maintain the same level of earnings.

11-2. *Involving Your Salespeople in Your Sales Meetings*

There are many advantages to getting your salespeople involved in your sales meetings. The most obvious reason is that this will keep them attentive and alert. They are more likely to learn and retain something from these sessions if they are a part of them. In college, I never fell asleep in a class in which I was a principal part, but I seldom made it through two hours of lecture, regardless of how interesting the topics were. Unless involved, your listeners may also feel that the idea you are trying to get across in your meeting is not directed at them, so they can concentrate on something else instead of what you are saying.

Another reason for involving your salespeople is that you learn more from seeing than from hearing, and you learn more from doing than from just seeing. One office I was associated with would bring in a telephone that was unplugged and have different agents respond to a floor duty inquiry. The advantages to this role playing were manyfold. First, the participants had to put some practice into their techniques before the sales meeting. Second, they gained greater confidence in their ability to use these techniques in a real floor duty situation, since there is no tougher audience than one containing your peers, especially when they know how the techniques are supposed to work and every obstacle that can cause you trouble. Third, each individual has an opportunity to see what does and does not work, so he or she can use the good points and avoid making the mistakes when on floor duty. By allowing your salespeople to critique the presentations of their associates, the entire group has the benefit of each others' ideas.

This same technique can be used for listing presentations with visual aids, telephone canvassing, overcoming objections, present-ing an offer, soliciting an offer from a potential buyer, and other aspects of selling real estate. The important thing is that your salespeople will come to your meetings prepared, will use the techniques you have taught them, and those not directly involved will have a chance to observe the best techniques in use. They will also open up and communicate their ideas with the rest of the group.

11-3. *Using Visual Aids to Enhance Your Sales Meetings and Keep Your Salespeople Interested*

The visual aid is badly neglected by most real estate sales managers, yet the effectiveness of this avenue of communication can be tremendous. The visual aid need not be of professional quality or expensive. Most times it can simply be printed on a paper easel.

The benefits of a visual aid and the purposes it serves are numerous. It provides an outline of your presentation, so your agents can take notes from it for future use. They can also have an idea of where the presentation is headed and relate what you are discussing to the overall impact the instruction can have on their ability to increase their income. A visual aid will also make the subject matter easier to understand and more interesting to the audience.

Use a visual aid in your sales meetings whenever possible. Your salespeople will be more impressed with your entire presenta-tion, simply because it looks more professional. And as already pointed out, people will remember what they saw long after they forget what they heard.

11-4. *"52" Sales Meetings that Will Generate Enthusiasm and Sales From Your Entire Staff*

On the following pages in this chapter, you will discover 52 different formats and outlines for successful, high-powered sales meetings. Each one is designed to fulfill the three goals of your sales meetings and to allow you to put on an effective presentation without spending hours preparing outlines, coming up with crea-tive ideas, and researching material. All you have to do is follow the format you are given by introducing material that is pertinent to your individual office and the needs of your salespeople.

Company Goal Review

Review the goals of your company for the next twelve months. Inform your agents of the dollar volume of sales you expect to reach this year and how it will affect them.

1. Growth.
2. Special projects such as: associating with a builder, promotions, new canvassing campaigns, etc.
3. What you need in dollar volume from each salesperson.
4. What you are going to do to enable each agent to reach that goal, such as changing office image, advertising budget, increased open houses, training, secretarial help, incentives, etc.
5. How reaching this goal will better the office, the individual, and your status in comparison to the competition.
6. Where your competition lies, and how as a unit you can beat them to reach your goal.
7. Open the floor for discussion. Ask the salespeople for their input on how you can reach the goal you have set and how they can be effective in doing what you have asked them.

FHA and VA Financing—Part One

Ask a local lender, perferably the most aggressive in your area, to attend your sales meeting and give a presentation on the present FHA and VA picture. His talk should include the following subjects:

A. Availability of FHA and VA funds.
B. Different programs he has available.
C. Present costs, including points, closing fees, etc.
D. Examples of what can be done with FHA and VA loans concerning credit, income, houses, unmarried buyers, co-signers, etc.
E. Handouts for each agent that include mortgage books, down payment schedules, heating and utility guidelines,

income leftover requirements for different-sized families, etc.

F. What appraisers are looking for and how to best ensure that you get a favorable appraisal.

G. How to appeal an appraisal and/or a rejected loan application.

H. Open the floor for questions and discussion. Have your agents prepare the questions in advance, so they will be able to take advantage of the expertise of your guest.

FHA and VA Financing—Part Two

Make any announcements you may have, and discuss how you feel the financing information they received today can be put to immediate use by recommending those listings that you feel would be suitable for FHA or VA financing. Also suggest how the salespeople might be able to find FHA and VA buyers, and give them advance notice of advertising you will be using to attract FHA and VA buyers.

Using Floor Duty Time Effectively

This presentation will include selecting two or three of your agents to use in a role-playing situation. Bring in a telephone and have one agent call in on an ad and another take the floor duty call. Ask the group to critique the good and bad points of each floor duty person's techniques.

Ask a representative from the local phone company to give a presentation on using the telephone effectively. They are the professionals of the do's and don't's of talking on the phone.

Ask two of your agents to use your "play" phone to canvass for a listing. I once had a sales manager who picked up a real telephone, randomly selected a name from the phone book, and proceeded to get an appointment for a listing presentation in the middle of our sales meeting. Either way, your salespeople will get some good ideas on how to use the telephone to solicit listings during their floor duty hours. Show them how to use the city directory, expired listings, the newspaper, and the telephone book to do random or area canvassing.

Discuss other suggestions for making their floor duty time productive, such as writing letters for a canvassing campaign, calling potential clients, etc. Also point out to them how much it costs you each time the telephone rings.

Listing Presentations

Ask two salespeople to give their listing presentations and two others to be potential sellers. This is particularly effective if your agents use visual aids in their presentations. The group will have an opportunity to compare the effectiveness of their presentations with that of the agents involved in the role-playing session and to discuss ideas on what has or hasn't been effective for them.

Carry your listing session a little further. Have another associate discuss price with the sellers, overcoming their objections and getting their signatures on a listing.

Listing Inventory Review

Go through all of your listings. Ask each listing agent to bring your sales staff up to date on their listings, including activity, seller's position, price, repairs, recent offers, or new financing terms. Give everyone an opportunity to comment on what they feel has been the problem with the property and their suggestions for moving it. Announce a listing contest for the upcoming week. The prizes might be $10 per listing, a balloon pop with cash prizes for each listing, a larger than normal commission for contest listings, a weekend trip for two, 100 gallons of gasoline, etc.

Motivational or Informative Films

Plan a film for this meeting. Your abstract company, title company, or Board of Realtors may have films you can borrow concerning listings, showings, canvassing, and many other subjects related to selling real estate. Many of these films come with a typed outline that you can copy and give to each of your agents. If the films are reasonably short, show two of them: one on canvassing and one on securing a listing, for instance.

Conclude your meeting with a group discussion on the films and how your agents can use the techniques they have just seen in their day-to-day selling.

Creative Real Estate Financing

Ask your best agent at financing to give a mini-seminar on financing real estate. Suggest that he or she not only review each avenue available to an agent and the best outlets for each type of loan, but also discuss examples of creative real estate financing and how it can be used to earn commissions.

Learning Appraisal Techniques

Invite an appraiser from a local loan company or your firm's certified appraiser to speak on appraisal techniques. This talk should include all three methods of appraising, as well as how and when to use each.

Open the floor for questions and discussion. Always be prepared to get the ball rolling by having your own questions ready if the agents are hesitant to get the discussion started.

Completing Contracts and Forms Correctly

Using an overhead projector, review each of your office's agreements and forms, point out the proper manner in which they should be completed, and highlight the errors that are most commonly made. Also, review the purpose of each of these forms and how they can be used to the agent's advantage, especially the Offer to Purchase and the Listing Agreement.

Salespeople's Meeting

Begin the meeting with only your agents present and give them the opportunity to discuss any subject they want among themselves, such as problems with management, policies, or changes they would like to see in the office.

Join the meeting at its midpoint and open the floor to any subject the agents would like to discuss, or suggest problems that management is having and changes that you feel are needed.

Buyer and Seller Motivation

Ask a local college professor in Psychology or an advertising executive to speak at your sales meeting and discuss reasons why people buy or sell. This discussion could deal with many of the aspects of motivation, such as: the reasons people want to own a home, how people make decisions, how to control different personalities, or the fears salespeople must overcome in buyers and sellers in order to get them to sign an agreement. Have your salespeople give some thought to the topic of the upcoming discussion, so they will be well prepared with questions for your speaker.

The New Home Market

Invite a builder to attend your sales meeting. His discussion should center on new home buying trends, the general price range of new homes, activity on the new home market, difficulties the builders face, what areas real estate salespeople can help in, the current availability of new home mortgage money, and the type of buyers generally in the new home market.

Your Growing Community

Ask a Chamber of Commerce representative to inform your agents on new activity in your community and where your community is headed. What new construction is underway or planned for the near future, and what new businesses have recently opened, expanded, or expect to do so soon. Is the community getting smaller or larger? How can your sales staff help the Chamber promote your community? What opportunities are present for the real estate agent?

Motivational Meeting

Get your salespeople enthused about selling. Review your goal after the first three months and determine what you need from your salespeople. Take a look at how you are gaining on the competition and how new policies in advertising or company image have affected sales. Use a visual aid to show them how they can earn an "X" amount of dollars by making "X" number of sales, which only requires "X" number of appointments, which can be obtained by "X" number of contacts. Show your agents how their total annual income is directly related to the number of contacts they make. Present a plan for each of them to follow for the next 30 days to increase their sales through increased activity on their part. Provide a checking system that will ensure they are following your plan without making it seem that someone is constantly looking over their shoulder.

Listing Ideas

Have your best listing agent give a presentation on where and how to get listings. Ask him to explain how he or she uses expired listings (his or her own, as well as the competitors'), moving companies, newspaper leads, bird dogs, canvassing, spot checking different neighborhoods, and industry contacts to get solid leads on listing candidates.

This agent might also explain how he or she initially gets a foot in the door, and how to get the owners to a point where they will sit down and listen to a listing presentation. Once the presentation has been completed, ask the rest of your staff to share some of their techniques for getting leads on potential sellers.

Salesperson's Choice

Survey your sales staff to see what they would like to discuss in this sales meeting and design the meeting to follow the choice of the majority of your agents. If you receive more than one idea (and you probably will), you can schedule other meetings to cover other subjects that would be beneficial and interesting to your agents.

Eliminating Legal Problems

Ask an attorney to speak to your sales staff on how to avoid legal problems as a real estate salesperson and the potential hazards that await them. Also ask him or her to explain the services an attorney provides and in which areas he or she can be of value to a real estate agent. He or she can also cover the areas that should be included in a fair and protective land contract, offer to purchase, and listing agreement.

Conventional Financing

Invite a savings and loan officer or bank official to explain the different types of residential and commercial real estate financing they have available and how they make determinations on credit applications and appraisals. You will want to make sure the following areas are included:

A. Closing costs

B. Normal time lapse from application to closings and what can cause delays

C. Minimum or maximum lending limits

D. Credit and income requirements

E. Lenders' attitude and aggressiveness on different types of buyers and properties

Seminar

If your office is not big enough to be able to afford a professional speaker, combine forces for one meeting with two or three other small offices and retain a speaker who is a professional in the field of selling real estate. A paid outside speaker will be more likely to impress your sales staff and cause the desired response from them.

Group Canvassing

If listings are down, use this week's session to canvass a neighborhood as a group. Divide the neighborhood into assigned blocks, allot the amount of time to be spent, and invade a high turnover area of your community.

For Sale by Owners

Prepare a presentation for your sales staff to reacquaint them with soliciting for sale by owners. Include in your talk areas such as:

A. Locating the for sale by owner
B. Three methods for contacting for sale by owners and the importance of timing
C. Dialogues your sales staff can use to get into the door
D. Using for sale by owners for buyer leads by getting a list of lookers who did not make an offer on the home
E. Giving a listing presentation to for sale by owners
F. Objections the for sale by owner will offer and counters your agents can use to overcome these objections
G. The importance of follow-up when attempting to secure a listing from a for sale by owner

Review Listing Inventory

It is once again time to review the status of your current listings. To put additional interest into this meeting, hold it at a local restaurant and discuss your inventory over breakfast.

Securing Out-of-Town Buyers

Put together a presentation designed to increase your agents' desire and ability to work with out-of-town buyers. Begin your presentation with a discussion of how beneficial these clients can be to an agent. Review the different ways an agent can get leads on new people moving into your community, such as industry contacts, newspaper leads on promotions and transferrees, motel and hotel contacts, and the Chamber of Commerce.

Point out the special needs of these buyers and how the agent must fulfill these needs. Actually run through the orientation and showing process, including an interview of the client's needs, a discussion of neighborhoods and price ranges, a tour of the city highlighting its attractions, and an information packet from the Chamber of Commerce.

Remind your sales staff of the importance of follow-up and the need for them to stick close to these clients until they have selected a home.

Developing an Investment Clientele

Investment property buyers are a gold mine to a real estate agent. Generally, they are always in the market to purchase a good investment property and will usually be willing to sell if the price or tax situation is right. Ask your investment property specialist to give a presentation on counseling and servicing the investment buyer. The topic should include:

A. Computing a return on an investment property

B. Understanding and dealing with the personality of investment buyers

C. What investment buyers are looking for in a property

D. Financing available for the investment buyer

E. Where to find investment property clients

Using Leasing Companies to Finance Sales

Leasing companies are an excellent source of financing when involved with a commercial transaction. They will buy the business from the seller, giving you your commission, and at the conclusion of the leasing period, turn title over to the buyer in accordance with previous arrangements. There are tax advantages to the buyer and it is normally easier to secure lease financing than bank financing. Ask a representative from the nearest leasing company to speak to your organization and explain how leasing works and how it can be used by your sales staff to earn commissions. Allow plenty of discussion time with this one.

Tour of Local Industry

Most industrial companies do allow tours of their facilities. Call several Personnel Managers and see if you can arrange a tour of their plants. Your agents will become more familiar with the products made by these companies and their organizational make-up. Both you and your salespeople will gain valuable contacts for future business by acquainting your office with people within these organizations.

Using Time Wisely

Ask one of your better organized salespeople to give the rest of your group some tips on using their time more efficiently. Include discussion on the value of an agent's time, where most time is wasted, and how much an agent can increase his or her earnings using effective scheduling of each day.

Goal Review

You are now half way through your year. Review with your agents your present status in comparison to the goal you set at the first of the year, congratulate them on their efforts, and explain what will be required to reach the plateau you have set. Ask for comments on what you can do to help them achieve your goal and explain what you already have planned to assist them in their efforts.

Trading Program

Review the activity generated by your trading program and the improvements you would like to see in the salespeople's efforts. Involve the salespeople in a discussion of the good and bad points in your program and any changes that need to be made. If necessary, review the workings of the program and highlight the advan-

tages to the salespeople offered by your plan. Discuss the successes
of your program up to this point.

Direct Mail Advertising

Compile a list of ways your agents can use direct mail to secure
buyers and sellers, become better known in your community, announce the advantages of your trading program, and prospect and
canvass for new clients. They can easily reach industry, apartment
dwellers, for sale by owners, newly married couples, neighborhoods with high turnover, and mobile home owners.

You should have a skeleton letter for each type of canvassing,
along with instructions on how the agent can get the addresses he
or she needs from the city directory.

Getting Listings Extended

Give a presentation on proven techniques for getting listings
extended and counters your agents can use to overcome the objections they are sure to hear. This is a good time to point out the need
for proper servicing of the listing during the listing period, and
good communication with the sellers from the very beginning.
Review this year's history of the percentage of listings extended;
the number of these that sold, earning the agents a commission;
and why it is essential to increase the number of listings being
extended by your agents.

Overcoming Objections

Select an agent or two in advance to counter objections offered
by buyers and sellers in each step of the selling process. Have
another agent play the role of the client offering objections in order
to see how effective your agents are in overcoming these objections
and getting the client back to making a decision.

Conclude with a group discussion and critique of the actors,
with the other agents offering their own techniques for responding
to the doubts of the client. Be prepared to offer tested, effective
counters for your staff to consider.

Discussion Time

Have an open format for this meeting. Encourage your staff
to discuss problems, inform them of questions that have arisen

lately and how they were answered and permit them to make suggestions on office policy changes and/or to comment on any aspect of the current real estate market. While no one likes problems, they are better aired and discussed than kept bottled up within a salesperson. This meeting also gives your salespeople an opportunity to compare notes and help each other with problems they are currently facing in real estate.

Listing Presentation

Since it has been several months since you reviewed your agents' listing presentation in a sales meeting, ask two of your newer associates to give their listing presentation. This will allow your staff to review any bad habits they have fallen into, and refresh their memory on the effectiveness of a well-constructed listing presentation. Allow for a discussion period and an opportunity for a group critique of the listing presentations given in the meeting.

Speaking to a Group

Most agents do not take advantage of the opportunities available to them to speak before groups. Encourage your salespeople to be more aggressive in this area by showing them how valuable this contact can be to their business, outlining the opportunities that are available to them, and giving them ideas of subjects on which they can speak. Include some tips on speaking before groups and the use of visual aids when giving a presentation.

Review Current Market Trends

Using visual aids, show your agents where the current real estate market is in terms of turnover compared to where it was a year ago, three years ago, and ten years ago. Explain the cycle of real estate sales and where the market is heading, not only in your community, but also nationwide. Give them some insight into what the near future holds for them and how they can take advantage of the current market trends and conditions.

Holding Successful Open Houses

By reviewing your records, determine your most effective salesperson at open houses. Ask him or her to explain the do's and don't's of conducting successful open houses, including:

A. Selecting the home
B. Advance publicity, such as neighborhood canvassing, signs, newspaper ads, and calls to prospects
C. Setting up the open house
D. Conducting the tour
E. Spotting the most likely prospects
F. Securing an offer

You should also have material available from publications or books that provides other successful techniques for holding profitable open houses. Announce a special open house effort for this weekend, and ask for each of your agents to hold an open house.

Motivational Meeting

Using one of the previously suggested sources, secure a motivational film on some aspect of selling real estate that is different from previous presentations.

Government Financing Avenues

Ask an official of the FHA and VA to visit your office to discuss the lesser known avenues available within his or her department. These would mostly be financing methods not handled by lenders, such as low income financing, large apartment or commercial projects, rehabilitation financing, etc. Ask the representative to bring any handout material he or she might have, along with information on interest rates, who qualifies, loan maturity, the process involved, and also some ideas on how your staff can use these financing methods to generate sales.

Small Business Administration

If you are familiar with the functions of the Small Business Administration, secure a complete set of forms used when making a loan application and instruct your salespeople on how SBA can help them with their commercial sales and the proper method of completing the forms and processing the application. If you are not familiar with this financing outlet, ask one of the SBA's representatives to speak to your staff. Either way, the session should include the following topics:

A. What the SBA does

B. The types of loans available through the SBA, either directly or through a guaranteed basis

C. Loan limits and qualifications required to receive an SBA loan

D. Completing the forms and processing the application

E. How to effectively use the SBA in their real estate business

F. Drawbacks and advantages to SBA financing

Goal Review

Three-fourths of your year is over. Update your staff on your actual situation compared to your projected goal, and explain what is required of each of them if you are to reach the standard you have set. This is the time for an all-out effort, so announce a contest for your agents. The prize could be for everyone if you reach a certain dollar volume or number of sales, or it could be for top producers within the next quarter. Since this will be a three-month drive, the reward should be substantial in order to keep your agents motivated.

Facts and Figures

This session can be used to motivate and inform, as well as provide your agents with some ammunition to use on prospective sellers. Include listings taken, listings sold, the average price of the homes sold, the average number of days listed before a home is sold, your percentage of the market, the average price of your current listings, the average difference in either percentage or dollars between listed price and sales price, the percentage or number of sales resulting from an open house, your percentage of increase over the previous year of sales, the average price of all homes currently listed in multi-list, and the average number of years before a home is resold.

Discuss what these facts and figures mean to the agent and how they can be effective when attempting to secure a listing, especially if there is competition. Ask for your staff's comments and views as to what these figures mean.

Evening Workshop

This type of meeting can be particularly effective if you have part-time salespeople or need a sales meeting that will last longer than usual. You can discuss office policies, have panel discussions or present two or three motivational films on canvassing, securing a listing, and showing the property.

Institutional Advertising for the Real Estate Agent

Give a presentation on how your agents can use institutional advertising to increase their business. Explain the purposes of institutional advertising and ideas on the best outlets to use, such as menus, moving companies, scorecards, motels, pens, calendars, playing cards, etc., and the costs involved in each method. If it is in your policy to do so, you can announce your firm's willingness to share in the expense. Include in your discussion examples of how this type of advertising has been effective in the past.

Review of Current Listings

Review your current inventory, giving each listing agent an opportunity to discuss the particular circumstances of the listing, the owners' needs, and any changes since the listing was taken. Encourage the other agents to comment or make suggestions concerning the listing.

By written ballot, select the top ten listings for your office, and announce the list to your staff. This will increase the incentive for the agents to secure buyers quickly for these listings because they will know that everyone else in the office has placed a high priority on these homes.

Buyer Interview Session

Ask two or three of your agents to participate in this week's session. Since buyers often fail to give an agent all of the information he or she needs or even factual information, it is helpful to practice interviewing buyers. The idea is to ask questions in such a way that the buyer's response must be more than a simple "yes" or "no," and in a manner that allows the agent to secure the information he or she needs, without offending the buyer or making him or her feel that the answer must be given in such a manner that produces a more positive picture than his or her actual circumstances warrant. The session will also be valuable in ensuring that all of your agents are aware of all of the information they must have from the buyer in order to be effective.

Farm and Rural Financing

Ask a representative from the Federal Land Bank and from the Farmer's Home Administration to discuss the financing methods they have availble, and how they can be useful to a real estate salesperson. Their talk should include discussion on loan costs, interest rates, eligibility, using their resources combined with other methods, and current mortgage money supply.

Tax Savings Through Real Estate

Invite a local accountant or CPA to discuss tax advantages available to real estate owners with your sales staff. Your sales staff will find new reasons for clients to buy or sell real estate due to tax savings. Subjects covered should include capital gains tax, tax liabilities on contract sales, advantages to trading, tax advantages for investment buyers, new tax credits for the home owner or buyer, etc.

Getting the Most from Your Newspaper

Plan a session that instructs your agents on the many leads presented to them in their daily newspaper. One effective way to do this is to cut out every lead in yesterday's paper and show the agents how the item could have meant a commission for them.

Encourage them to present their ideas on how to increase the number of leads they can get from the newspaper and tips on what has been effective for them. Now cut out every possible lead from today's paper, assign each of your salespeople an even number of leads to follow up on, and ask them to report back at the next sales meeting as to the response they received from these leads. Your paper should be nothing but holes by the time you cut out for sale by owners, rent ads, promotions, transfers, deaths, births, marriages, announcements of expansion, news of shutdowns, notices of bankruptcy, retirements, announcements of resignations for social positions, garage sales, etc.

Review of Newspaper Leads

What was the response from your agents' activities? What type of leads proved the most worthwhile to follow up? How did the agents approach the lead and how did they follow up once contact was made? Did they follow the same practice with the newspaper for the remainder of the week? Had the competition been there yet?

Canvassing Techniques

With the assistance of one of your salespeople, give a presentation on canvassing for buyers and sellers. Prepare dialogues to be used when canvassing door-to-door, by telephone, or with letters. Use the numbers game to show your staff the effect canvassing can have on the volume of their business. Just as important, point out to them the type of neighborhoods that show the best response to canvassing. A neighborhood with little turnover will be in high demand with your agents' clients, but if few sellers are available, they will be wasting their time and efforts canvassing the area. Proven high turnover areas are the most productive for real estate salespeople, and they should remember that their goal is high volume activity, not one listing from weeks of canvassing efforts.

Advertising Ideas

As you conclude this year and look towards next year, get input from your salespeople as to what they feel has been the most effective advertising campaign of the year and their ideas for new advertising campaigns.

Which type of advertising brought them the most responses and which type produced the best leads? Was the overall response worth the advertising dollars you invested? Were there any advertising campaigns that the agents felt were particularly ineffective? In what area would they like to see an increase in their advertising budget?

11-5. Increasing Sales with Professional Sales Meetings

Presented properly, these sales meetings will provide you with a staff of highly motivated, aggressive salespeople using proven selling techniques. Your agents' morale, attitude towards your weekly meetings, and degree of professionalism will increase considerably, simply because you have created this type of atmosphere with your sales meetings. Even though pressing demands are placed on your time, over the long run, nothing you do will be as important as your sales meetings. They are your opportunity to develop an entire staff of enthused and knowledgeable real estate salespeople. The earnings generated for your office as a result of high-powered sales meetings will make the effort required on your part worthwhile

12

Supervising
A Successful
Real Estate Staff

Supervising another individual requires the ability to bring out the best in that person, while at the same time giving him or her enough leadway to perform in a manner that feels comfortable and respectable. No control promotes poor morale and chaos. Tight controls deter creativity and initiative. As sales manager, you often have to walk the fine line between supervising and governing.

No group of people is harder to supervise than real estate salespeople due to their very nature, and they require unique supervising techniques. Chapter Twelve discusses some of the problems incurred in supervising a professional sales staff and how you can overcome them. You will consider how you can help your salespeople increase their income (and yours), while at the same time avoid limiting an agent's need for independence and self-initiative.

12-1. Ensuring that Your Salespeople Use Their Time Wisely

One of the most important areas where you can have an impact on a salesperson is the use of his or her time. You can regulate this commodity in several ways that we will discuss later in this chapter, but one of the first steps you must take is to put emphasis on the value of using one's time productively. Unless

227

your agents understand the importance of time management and your support of it, they won't be concerned about implementing productive time-utilization techniques.

Real estate salespeople will tell their spouses, their friends, their children, and even their sales manager that they work 12–14 hours a day, seven days a week selling real estate. In reality, they spend two or three productive hours each day actively earning a living. The remainder of their time is spend doing legal work, checking on closings, sitting on floor duty reading the paper, drinking coffee in their favorite stop, talking with fellow agents, and "talking real estate" with unproductive sources.

Every hour that goes by is an opportunity lost forever if a real estate salesperson is not showing a property to a qualified candidate, giving a listing presentation, or making calls on new prospects. He or she might as well take $20 and throw it in the trash, because that is what an unproductive hour has cost. Time is the only limit to a salesperson's income. Time, like oil to industry, is his or her limited and nonrecyclable resource.

You can help your salespeople ensure that they use their time wisely by showing them how to make the best use of it, and by carefully watching how they utilize their most precious commodity. If they know they have to account to you for each hour, they will put more emphasis on using it productively. I would much rather my salespeople spent two hours sitting at home or out fishing than at lunch with other salespeople, or doing paperwork in the office. At least they would be relaxing, which is much more productive than loafing.

12-2. *Limiting Your Demands on Your Agents' Time*

Before you begin preaching to your salespeople about making the best use of their productive time, make sure you are not one of the "time stealers" yourself. There are certain requirements you must place on their time. By doing so, you are ensuring them of higher productivity and higher earnings. You would be doing them a disservice if you did not require them to meet certain criteria, such as sales meetings, tours of homes, floor duty, completion of various forms, and training sessions. These are all required to maintain a high degree of productivity and professionalism.

There are other demands, however, that are often placed on

real estate agents' time by their sales managers that are non-productive and create part of the very problem you want to eliminate. They include, but are not limited to, lengthy sales meetings, canvassing projects, long and unnecessary forms, ad writing, and too frequent counseling sessions. These time-drainers encourage the nonproductive use of time, and put you in a position of contributing to the very practice you want to eliminate.

Survey the demands you place on your agents' time. Are they really necessary and do they increase your agents' ability to make sales? Are they the most productive use of your agents' time? You should not only look at the amount of time you require from your salespeople, but more importantly, are you stealing productive hours from them? Certain hours are best designated for showing property, listing presentations, or prospecting for new business. There are only a few of these hours in each day, and they shouldn't be misused for nonproductive or less important functions.

12-3. Encouraging Effective Time Management

A common error among real estate salespeople is the misappropriation of their time. They work on closings when they should be showing property. They are making calls when they should be giving a listing presentation. They are prospecting when people are least receptive to being interrupted. There are certain times that must be reserved for specific activities. Your agents' day must be planned for the convenience of those they hope to serve. The following is a guideline for you to use in helping your agents determine the most effective use of their time. It is designed to increase their chances of finding prospects receptive to their calls and making the maximum use of their productive time.

Early Morning	Perform duties required on pending transactions. Review new listings and multi-list information. Compile canvassing letters and schedule for the remainder of the day.
10:00A.M.–12:00P.M.	Canvass door-to-door and on the telephone. Make calls on for sale by owners. Contact prospects on the agents' monthly list. Make appointments with second shift workers.

12:00P.M.–1:00P.M.	Have lunch with businessmen, industrial contacts, clients or lenders.
1:00P.M.–3:00P.M.	Call on business people and industry contacts. Call on for sale by owners. Service listings.
3:00P.M.–8:00P.M.	Have showing appointments.
8:00P.M.–?	Give listing presentations. Present offers.

Psychologically, this schedule utilizes the most advantageous timing for finding people receptive. Each is designed to find the prospect in the best possible mood to devote his or her attention to your agents.

12-4. Ensuring Your Own Schedule Is 100% Productive

Just as it is imperative to the success of the agent for him or her to make the most productive use of time, it is also imperative to the success of your office that you, as sales manager, practice time-efficient management techniques. If you allow yourself to spend more time on duties that do not require your personal attention or are unproductive than you do on those areas that can generate more income for your salespeople and your office, you are committing a bigger sin than your inefficient agent, because your responsibilities are much larger.

Below is a suggested schedule for the most efficient and productive use of your time.

8:00A.M.–9:00A.M.	Begin each morning with a quick review of your pending file. Write notes to those agents who should follow-up on something today, or ask about their status.
10:00A.M.–12:00P.M.	Individual sales meeting with agents, follow-up on personal sales, meet with media salespeople and ad agencies, outside salespeople, in-office training, etc.
Lunch	If you do not have an appointment for lunch with a lender, builder, chamber of commerce person, etc., take one of your agents to lunch.

1:30P.M.–3:00P.M.	Write or review advertising, develop sales meetings, budget, attend closings, review agents' production, develop motivational programs, solve problems, etc.
3:00P.M.–5:00P.M.	In-field training or supervision of agents. If this time slot is not filled by this activity, use it to show or meet with your own clients and make calls on new clients.
Evening Hours	Leave your salespeople alone and get out of the office! Your salespeople should be using this time to earn commissions. If you stay in the office on a regular basis in the evening, you become stale. If you have a special project or paperwork, take them home. Use this time to work with your own clients, plan tomorrow's activities, or hopefully relax, but don't—don't—use it as training, meeting, or office time.

Just as important as planning your time carefully is the use of that time. Carefully consider your responsibilities. Which ones might be as easily performed by a secretary or by the agents themselves? Can someone else write the ads after you have trained them, with you simply reviewing them weekly? Can someone else prepare the floor duty roster, compile records, and maintain agents' files? Is it necessary that you attend closings, take floor duty, or deal with outside vendors? Even if you believe you must perform these duties, give them up for a week or a month and compare the results. As you tell your agents, never say something won't work until you try it.

12-5. Eliminating "Time Stealers"

There are many "time stealers" practiced by real estate salespeople, either intentionally or accidentally. As sales manager you must be on the watch for these practices and ready to put an end to them. Many are hidden behind good intentions and seemingly productive activities. The bottom line at the end of the month will tell you if your agent is using effective time management or employing costly "time stealers." Following is a list of areas requiring your supervision:

12-5A. Office Time

Is the agent actually working when he's in the office, or is he merely shuffling papers? Are the calls he's making or the analysis he is developing productive and necessary?

12-5B. Canvassing

Canvassing is important and an excellent method of producing leads, but is your agent utilizing effective canvassing techniques? Does he or she have a presentation when knocking on a door, or making a call? Is he or she canvassing a productive area, or one that rarely produces a listing?

12-5C. Schedule

Real estate salespeople can only make the most effective use of every minute of their time if they know in advance what they will be doing with their day. If your agents are unorganized, or their day is unplanned, they will waste valuable, productive time. They must also stick to their schedules and not let prospects rearrange their day. It is tempting to cancel a planned activity to run out and show a property but, in the long run, the agents become like the lion that starts chasing one game, and repeatedly switches to another that catches his eye. Soon, he is worn out and still hungry because he didn't catch any of them.

12-5D. Non-Qualified Clients

An agent must initially follow-up on every lead. Anyone can buy a house if they are willing to take the action necessary to secure a home. A danger that waits for agents, though, is working too long with prospects who have no real intention of buying a home or selling a property, or who are not willing to be realistic with their requirements in a home. Even if the agent eventually succeeds and secures an agreement, the hours he or she has devoted are not justified by the commission received.

12-5E. Other Salespeople

A certain amount of association between salespeople is healthy and necessary. Time spent exchanging ideas, experiences, and techniques can be very productive. However, time spent in excess drinking coffee, going to lunch, or telling war stories is nonproductive, since it is doubtful that one agent can sell another a home.

12-5F. Prospecting

This important element of selling can be turned into a negative factor if time is spent on people the agent knows and who have been nonproductive in the past. It is easy to fall into a pattern of making calls on people you know, since there is no pressure and you can be assured of a receptive response, but more than an occasional contact is wasting time that could be spent making new contacts.

12-6. Instituting Time-Saving Techniques

Since salespeople's time is their most important and limited resource, they must develop techniques that ensure the fullest utilization of their time. I have included some simple time-saving techniques practiced by successful real estate agents to obtain the most productivity in the least amount of time. You should encourage your salespeople to incorporate these procedures into their daily routine.

12-6A. Floor Duty

Floor duty time should be used for much more than waiting for the phone to ring. Average salespeople view this time as three hours taken from their schedule, while successful salespeople see it as an opportunity to increase activity. Your salespeople should be using their floor duty hours to make prospecting calls, construct market analyses, call on for sale by owners, write canvassing letters, arrange appointments, and follow-up on closings.

12-6B. Pending Transactions

Productive time is wasted picking up abstracts, ordering deeds, taking legal work to lenders, and ordering inspections. These details can be handled by abstract companies, secretaries, or attorneys. They do not require the personal attention or professional expertise of the agent. Whenever an agent has an opportunity for someone else to do his or her legwork, he or she should take it. The agent's time is better spent putting together another transaction.

12-6C. Showing Technique

Time spent showing property can be reduced if an agent does his or her homework beforehand. If he or she knows what the buyers want and need in a home, and what homes are available, a real estate salesperson should be able to obtain an offer with three showings. Assuming that he or she has scheduled the properties in the proper order, the buyers will be convinced of the home they want at the conclusion of viewing the third property.

12-6D. Prospecting and Canvassing

Salespeople have a tendency not to plan their prospecting and canvassing activities. Instead, they attempt to utilize time that has not been planned for anything else to make these calls. To ensure productive and time-conservative prospecting and canvassing activity, an agent must set aside a certain amount of time each day, and plan the area he or she will be developing.

12-7. Keeping Your Top Producers in the Fold

Supervising a successful staff of real estate salespeople demands more than just a watchful eye on how they utilize their time. Real estate salespeople, particularly good ones, are unique in their psychological make-up. A sales manager must walk a fine line to ensure that he or she is supervising them and answering their needs without stifling those traits that make the individual successful. Motivating and training an average salesperson is as difficult as the task of keeping your top producers in line and happy at the same time.

A successful agent can easily become a prima donna if you allow it to happen. If they begin to work outside of the rules or feel that they deserve special treatment, the morale of your agents will deteriorate. On the other hand, if you do not recognize an agent's special talents or success, his or her ego will require him or her to look elsewhere for recognition. You can avoid these conflicts by providing ego boosters for your top salespeople, while making it clear that office policy dictates that all agents follow certain procedures.

You can answer the needs of these individuals by sponsoring "Salesperson of the Month" awards, giving additional advertising space based on volume, allotting secretarial time based on production, and personally recognizing their achievements during your monthly meetings. As mentioned earlier, a bonus system is one of the best means of rewarding your top producers and giving them an incentive to remain with your office.

Occasionally, salespeople need to be reminded of why they have been successful in the past. They attended sales meetings, used proven floor duty techniques, used professional listing presentations, and utilized the forms and records you required them to complete. They must also be mature enough to realize that their attitude and activities affect the morale of the other salespeople on your staff.

12-8. Handling the Problem Salesperson

Discontent and disobedience cannot be tolerated if your office is to succeed. When agents begin to dwell on the negative aspects of your company or feel they no longer have to follow the rules, your structure will begin to fall apart. This situation normally develops because of the actions of one agent, then spreads to your entire staff. To prevent poor morale from tearing down your organization, you have to stop a problem salesperson before he or she can influence others. You also have an obligation to show your staff that mavericks will not be tolerated.

Before you can take the appropriate action to bring a salesperson under control, you must evaluate the underlying factors that are causing the problem. Can they be corrected, and if so how?

If they can't be corrected, is the problem serious enough to force you to sever your association with the individual? Does the agent possess enough potential to make the time and effort you must devote to correcting the situation worthwhile?

Because of the ease agents have in associating with other offices, sales managers have a tendency to tolerate actions they know are damaging to their operation. If you stop and consider, this shouldn't be a concern, since it would be to your advantage to have the agent creating havoc among your competitors. Following are some steps you can take to salvage the agent and the success of your operation at the same time, before you let him loose on your competition.

A. Closer supervision—You may be able to get the agent back into the groove if he or she knows you are going to be working with him or her closely for a period of time.

B. Counseling—Discuss the problems the agent has been experiencing and the difficulties they have caused you. Offer your assistance in solving the problem or aiding the agent.

C. Motivation—Most problem salespeople have lost their motivation and are looking for someone or something else to blame for their failures. This person must be re-motivated with tapes, written material, and incentives.

D. Guidelines—Let the agent know early where he or she stands and what is expected in order to continue to be associated with your office. This step should be taken early, before the agents' poor habits have become too deep-seated to be changed.

E. Restrictions—As a last resort, restrict the privileges afforded the agent, such as doing floor duty, being named in the paper and having open hours until such time as he or she begins practicing the techniques and procedures required of all your agents. While this places more emphasis on phasing out the agent than rehabilitating him, it will serve as notice to your other agents that everyone must follow the rules. People expect and want justice. They do not want to see people continually break the rules without suffering. While you will probably lose an agent, you will have saved a productive staff.

12-9. *Evaluating the Potential of Each Salesperson*

Some criteria must be used to determine the potential of each salesperson, what steps you must take to increase his or her earnings, and how much time you can afford to devote to this person, considering the income he or she will bring into your office. Supervising salespeople is in one respect like selling property. The lower the value of the home, the less commission you will earn, and the harder you will have to work to bring the transaction to a close. With salespeople, the lower their volume, the more supervision they will require to maintain their level of income. At some point, however, as with selling homes, the commissions earned by the agents no longer justifies the time and effort you must devote to enable them to earn an income. If you have been unable to increase someone's potential, you must then accept the fact that the person's present level of income is the best he or she is going to do, and draw the line on how much time you are willing to give to the salesperson. Too often, sales managers spend 80 percent of their time supervising salespeople who earn only 25 or 30 percent of their office's income.

Your time should be devoted to those areas where you can most effect an increase in productivity. After determining an agent's potential, compared with his or her present income, consider how many hours you have to devote to supervision. Using the formula that follows, you can effectively determine the amount of supervisory time you should spend with each agent.

Depending on which area of your agent's selling technique needs attention, you may or may not be able to succeed with the amount of supervisory time that your formula indicates should be

Potential Income	$30,000
Present Income	$22,000
Potential Increase	$ 8,000
Total Office Potential Increase	$94,000
Percent of Office Potential Increase for Salesman	8.5%
Supervisory Time Allotment	8.5%

allotted. Each agent is an individual, who will learn at a different pace and respond to different motivations. But if you find that you have strayed too far from your schedule, you are not being as productive with your time as you must to achieve maximum potential. Time spent with one agent takes away from time that can be spent with another agent, thus reducing his or her potential. The responsibility of a sales manager is to juggle time to ensure a fair allotment that enables each salesperson to reach his or her maximum potential.

12-10. *Understanding What's Important to Real Estate Salespeople*

Just as we may perceive our office image differently than does the public, as sales managers we also often have a different perception of what our salespeople want from us. A recent survey points out how little sales managers really understand the needs and goals of their salespeople. On the left is a list of sales managers' priorities for their salespeople. The right column is a list of the salespeople's own priorities.

Sales Manager's Concept	Salespeople's Concept
1. Good wages	1. Appreciation
2. Job security	2. Feeling part of the team
3. Promotion and growth	3. Assistance
4. Good working conditions	4. Job security
5. Work interest	5. Good wages
6. Personal loyalty	6. Work interest
7. Discipline	7. Promotion and growth
8. Appreciation	8. Personal loyalty
9. Assistance	9. Good working conditions
10. Feeling part of the team	10. Discipline

It is easy to see why many sales managers have trouble reaching their salespeople. If your supervisory efforts are directed towards your concept of what your agents want, rather than what they feel is important, you cannot fully motivate them. Instead of increasing their potential with your efforts, you will be frustrating your agents' efforts to reach their goals.

12-11. *Building on the Strength of Your Salespeople*

There are two types of people management: negative management and positive management. Negative management places emphasis on the agent's weaknesses and uses negative incentives. Instead of using rewards as incentives, salespeople are encouraged to improve through threats of failure, discipline, or discharge if their weaknesses are not strengthened.

Positive management, on the other hand, attacks the strengths of your salespeople. You teach your agents to utilize their strengths to overcome their weaknesses. Animal trainers have known for years that animals respond quicker and correctly when they use positive rewards rather than negative ones in teaching them. People will also respond quicker when the same techniques are employed.

List each of your agent's strengths. Beside each strength, list your strategy for building on that strength and helping the agent use it to reach the highest income possible. Now, list each of your agent's weaknesses. Consider how you can use an agent's strength to overcome a weakness. You cannot ignore weaknesses. That's not what positive management means. You must inventory them, evaluate how to overcome them, and encourage your agents to turn them into strengths. Ignoring them will neither make them go away, nor make the agent stronger. You can, however, turn a weakness into a strength without placing emphasis on the weakness.

Assume you have an agent who obtains more than an average number of offers and always seems to have a good number of clients, but whose listing inventory is always down. The agent either fails to place emphasis on listings or is not a good lister. By pointing out how good he or she is with buyers and encouraging him or her to use the same techniques with sellers, you can use a strength to overcome a weakness. They both require the same basic technique: discovering leads and asking for the agreement.

People respond to praise and appreciation. They withdraw from criticism and failures. They make excuses to protect their own egos, and to stave off the criticism of others. Good managers know this fact and utilize positive management techniques to prevent their people from developing excuses, eventually convincing themselves of their innocence. An example of how positive management can be employed effectively occurred the other day in my own family. My oldest son is the point guard on his basketball team. They were undefeated until they lost a game by only two points that they should have won. My son's statistics were as good as usual but it was obvious to me as I watched the game that he was not playing with his usual intensity. It was not something you could put your finger on, but he wasn't making things happen as he usually did. They shouldn't have lost the game, and I expected the coach to give him a good chewing out in the locker room. When he came out, he was, of course, disheartened. He knew he had cost the team the game as much as anyone else, and he knew he was the one looked upon for the big play when it was needed.

"I don't think I'll start tomorrow night," he said.

"Why," I asked, "Did the coach get on you?"

"He didn't say anything to me," he replied. "If I have a good game he tell's me I played well, but if I have a bad game, he doesn't say anything to me."

Sure enough, for the first time in his life, Larry didn't start in the next basketball game. When he did go in half-way through the second quarter, the team was down by six points. By the end of the game, he had scored more points than in any other game of the year, and the team won without any difficulty. For the remainder of the year, his intensity was as great as it had ever been. The coach had been successful getting Larry back on track for two reasons. First, he used praise for motivation rather than fear. Second, he didn't give Larry a chance to make excuses for his performance. There were none, so why give him an opportunity to convince himself that the failure was the fault of someone else. As sales managers, we should employ the same style of management when working with our salespeople.

13

Developing
A Trading Program
That Will Increase
Both Sales and Profits

Normally, when you increase sales, you can also expect to increase profits. When implementing a trading program, however, the two do not necessarily go hand-in-hand. Many trading programs drain the profits of real estate offices, since you are actually gambling on the home market when you purchase a property to enable your agents to earn a commission on another home. And any gamble contains an element of risk. Several aggressive real estate offices have devised programs, however, that allow them to compete in the trade market while reducing the risk factor they must accept. Since this is the goal of every sales manager, Chapter Thirteen presents you with the format of four such programs.

Before we review these proven money makers, let's quickly consider what a trading program can and cannot do for your firm and the difficulties you will encounter.

13-1. Benefits of a Successful Trading Program

Offices that don't have an active trade program downplay the benefits they have to offer the seller. In the process, they often convince themselves that trading programs are not beneficial to the seller or the office. Realistically, however, a trading program *is* necessary to be competitive with other real estate offices in your community. Your program can also be a profitable service, rather than a liability if handled properly. Some of the benefits you will enjoy include:

A. Eliminating the edge your competition has on you.

B. Overcoming the constant problem of buyers who must sell before they buy, but won't list until they find another home.

C. Increasing the number of buying prospects for your office by being able to advertise your trade program.

D. Increasing the number of attractive listings, which attracts more buyers and sellers.

E. Increasing office profits by earning money on equity as well as commissions.

F. Motivating your salespeople to talk to buyers and sellers, and most importantly, *sell.*

If you could put together a trading program with your available resources and not lose any money, you'd do it, wouldn't you? In all honesty, every objection to a trading program by a sales manager reduces itself to capital required and a loss of profits. If you could be assured of not needing a lot of capital or losing money, you'd be happy, even if you didn't make a profit. Add to that the benefits you can receive, and a trading program becomes very attractive.

13-2. *Avoiding the Pitfalls that Await Your Trading Program*

Obviously, if all were rosy with trading programs, every office would have one. There are many areas that can bog down your program and keep it from ever getting off of the ground. By recognizing them in advance, however, you can avoid the profit stealers that destroy most trading programs. Following is a list of the four major pitfalls to avoid:

13-2A. *Your Staff*

Yes, the biggest problem you will encounter is your own sales staff. With a potential commission on the line, your agents will tend to see more potential in a property than is actually present. First, you must have a conservative appraisal and not one inflated by the unconscious desire for the property to be worth more. Second, if because of your conservative appraisal, the transaction cannot be put together, you will develop hard feelings between the agent, who has now been put in a spot with the sellers, and the office. To avoid this problem, you must use an appraiser who is not involved with the transaction and your agents must understand the mechanics and dollars and cents of your program.

13-2B. Area

The three factors that determine the salability of a property is location, location, and location. This is especially true if you are the one who will be trying to quickly turn a property over in order to reduce your exposure. A good location isn't necessarily the criteria for your purchase. The location must be one that turns over quickly, or you must build in the expense of paying several months of interest and upkeep.

13-2C. Timing

A home that has already been on the market six months or a year will be very difficult to move quickly, regardless of any price reduction or repairs you might make. The stigma of being for sale for an extended period of time will remain with the property.

13-2D. Market Evaluation

You have to be able to foresee the near future as well as accurately evaluate the present market. Is the market on the upswing or the downswing? Will the money market be better or worse in two months? Most failures are due to failure to consider the market over the next few months. Real estate offices take a home on trade under present market conditions, but if the market changes in a month or two, they haven't built in reserves to cope with the market. If you fail to consider the short term future market, you may end up holding a home for twelve months instead of two, or having to sell the property for less than you anticipated.

13-3. Why Trading Programs Fail

Trading programs that are not successful fail for one of two reasons. The office offers too much for the property, in which case they lose money, or else they offer too little for the property and the transaction is never made, and they lose a commission. While the latter is less costly than the former, it is still a failure because no money or sales are made, which puts your program out of contention with your competitors.

Forget all other factors. These two errors account for all trading program failures in the end. While many factors contribute, such as poor market, tight money, or the condition of the property, in the final analysis, the broker paid too much for the property under the circumstances, or else failed to obtain the property by being too conservative with his or her appraisal.

Jim R., a broker, agreed to guarantee the sale of a property at $56,900 if it hadn't sold within twelve months. The home was marketed at $59,900 until the last month prior to the broker purchasing the property, when it was reduced to $57,999. After one year on the market, the property hadn't sold and Jim found himself faced with $600 per month interest payments. There was no way for him to break even. He realized mid-way through the guarantee period that, if the property didn't move at $3,000 more than he was going to pay for it, he was in trouble, but by then it was too late to prevent the mistake. He was stuck purchasing a property that had already had a "For Sale" on it for twelve months. By the time he finally sold the property, he not only had lost his commission, but he also lost over $2,000 of his own money.

Under pressure from his salespeople, Robert M. put together a trade program that he felt would protect him from losses suffered by the other office. On his first trade offer, he agreed to pay fifteen percent less than the appraised value for the property. He then deducted a trading fee, a commission, interest for six months, taxes, insurance, and upkeep. Not only did the seller-buyer not accept the trade offer, but he also took his business elsewhere, which cost the salesperson and the office two commissions. After several attempts similar to the first, the agents refused to even suggest a trade with their clients, the broker had offended several clients, and the program was a complete failure.

How can you be assured of not paying too much for a property, yet paying enough to make the transaction work? First, you should use an outside appraiser who can be more objective because he or she is not involved in the transaction. Second, consider the four pitfalls that await your program, as listed in Section 13-2. Deduct a reasonable amount for expenses, but don't try to over-protect yourself at the expense of the seller.

13-4. Costly Mistakes that Can Steal Your Profit

Most mistakes are oversights or failures to correctly evaluate costs, market, or the effect certain aspects of a property have on its value or salability. Following is a list of areas that should be considered when reviewing a trade:

A. Structural Soundness—Don't guess, know! Ask for inspections for termites, the heating system, the plumbing, the electrical system, the basement, the septic tank, the well and the roof.

B. Market—Determine the maximum selling time and deduct the interest costs for that period.

C. Condition—Consider the property vacant. How will it show? What faults are the furniture hiding?

D. Independent Appraisal—Don't base your decision on your conservative estimate or your agent's optimistic estimate.

E. Minor Expenses—Little items count when they are whittling away at your profit. Items to be considered include taxes, insurance, lawn care, cleaning, utilities, heat, closing costs when sold, inspections, and minor repairs.

F. Interest Rates—When you make a offer, consider changes in interest rates or lock the rate in at that time. One broker I know guaranteed a home when the interest rates were 11 percent. By the time he had to purchase the property, *the rates had jumped to 14 percent.* His margin for error was eaten up very quickly by the increased cost of money.

G. Cushion—Real estate is not a science. Even the best of guesses will miss from time to time. If you are too conservative, the sellers will not accept your guarantee, but you can't ask full market value either. Three percent of the appraised value should be deducted to provide you a sufficient margin.

H. Reserve Fund—There will still be homes that cost you money. A percentage of each commission and/or profit from a trade should be placed in reserve to cover losses incurred on other trade transactions.

13-5. *Four Profit-Producing Trading Programs and How They Can Work for You*

Through my association with large and small offices throughout the country, I have found four trading programs that, while quite different, are equally profitable for their offices. These proven, successful programs are designed to motivate both the seller and the salespeople.

13-5A. *Three-Home Trade*

This program is extremely effective for offices with small amounts of capital and available cash flow. The fundamentals are simple, and provide a higher net than usual for the sellers. The principle behind this program is that, by involving three commissions, additional capital isn't required and there is enough cushion that each agent takes a reduced commission, at worst.

Buyer B makes an offer on Property A, subject to Buyer B's home selling within 30 days. Buyer B then lists his property with your office. You secure a buyer for his home who must also sell a home before completing the purchase, so Buyer C makes an offer on Property B subject to you purchasing property C. The office purchases Property C at full appraised value, minus anticipated expenses and a commission. This allows the other two transactions to close, so you now have commissions for Properties A, B, and C. Each salesperson involved, as well as the office, leaves their share of the commissions to be used to make the purchase and cover expenses, until Property C has been sold. At that time, the commissions are divided, according to interest in the transaction and the actual net returned.

Commissions and Available Shares

Property	Sales Price	Selling Agent	Listing Agent	Office Comm.
Property A	$80,000	LS-$1680	PM-$1680	$2240
Property B	$65,000	JB-$1365	LS-$1365	$1620
*Property C	$50,000	PM-$1050	JB-$1050	$1400

The sales price* represents the amount paid by the office for the property. The listing agent will be the agent who secured the offer on Property B and actually brought the third party into the transaction. Since the property has not yet sold, the selling commission is not allotted.

Available capital from three commissions	= $13,450.
Down payment required on purchase—$50,000 @ 20%	= $10,000.
Balance available for expenses & cushion	= $ 3,450.

Three months after your purchase the property, you sell the home for $51,000. Your expenses were as follows:

Additional Commission to the Selling Agent (Selling Agent does not share in any loss/profit)	$ 21.
Interest for 3 Months	1,200.
Closing Costs	1,000.
Insurance	40.
Upkeep	75.
Total Expense of Transaction	2,336.
Net	48,664.
Loss on Transaction	1,336.
Commission Fund after Selling Agent's Commission	12,400.
Amount Available for Distribution	$11,064. or 89.23%

(continued)

Distribution of Commissions

LS -89.23% of 3,045.00	= $ 2,717.05
PM -89.23% of 1,680.00	= $ 1,499.05
JB -89.23% of 2,415.00	= $ 2,154.90
Office -89.23% of 5,260.00	= $ 4,693.00
Total Paid Out	**$11,064.00**

Profits made are distributed in the same manner. If a reserve fund is maintained, two percent should be deducted from the top of the commission fund before distribution.

13-5B. Guaranteed Sales—87 Percent

The simplest of the four trading programs, the 87 percent program requires a greater availability of capital, but it is neat, clean, and leaves enough room to protect your office from loss. When the seller finds the home they want, the broker buys their home in order to release their equity, paying them 87 percent of appraised value.

Appraised Value	$93,000.
Commission	6510.
Loan Fee and Closing	2790.
Cushion	2790.
Cash to Seller	80,910.

The seller is guaranteed this amount if the property doesn't sell within sixty days. If the home is well priced, the owner has an excellent chance of selling the property within that sixty-day period, and at a higher amount than the guarantee. In the meantime, the home the seller is buying is taken off the market.

13-5C. Trading Company

Another proven, successful trade program is the formation of a trading company. The operation would carry your business name, but be identified as a trading company such as "Lone Star Real Estate Trading Co." This particular program is the most complicated of the four, and is more difficult to sell to both the buyer and the seller since it requires a commitment from both. It does protect the broker, however, and with a few adjustments can be simplified if desired.

One of your agents has a buyer willing to purchase a property you have listed, if you will purchase his home. You secure an independent appraisal or an appraisal from a member of your staff under contract to the trading company. After receiving his appraisal, you make a full-priced offer (or actually your trading company makes him an offer), contingent upon the following agreement:

1. Seller-Buyer will pay a 7 percent commission.
2. Seller will pay a 3 percent trading fee.
3. All anticipated expenses are deducted.
4. Seller of home being purchased by Seller-Buyer will also pay a 3 percent trading fee, plus a 7 percent commission.
5. The property will be placed on the market for 90 days prior to purchase by the trading company.
6. The purchaser pays for the appraisal on his property.

13-5D. *Guaranteed Sale*

This program is used by many brokers to encourage activity and get the edge on the competition in listings. In short, the property is listed with the guarantee that if it hasn't sold by the expiration date, the broker will purchase the property at a previously agreed upon price.

The key to successfully using this program is your ability to initially get the property on the market at a reasonable price. If it is grossly overpriced early, not only will you have to buy the property, but you will also be stuck with it for a longer period of time because of the initial reaction of the buying market.

13-6. *Setting Up Your Personal Trading Program*

The mechanics of establishing a trade program can be as simple or as complicated as you like, depending on the program you choose. If you utilize a separate company for your program, you will have additional tax filings, separate accountings, and incorporation for protection. This is not necessarily bad, just something you should consider.

The following steps are necessary to develop your own trade program:

A. Financial—Before you market a trading program, you must know that you can arrange financing, the cost of financing, and the terms available to you. Meet with the lender most likely to cooperate with you and get a commitment on what they will do for you.

B. Evaluate Competition—For your program to be effective, it must also be competitive. If you can't better the competition, or at least match them, your program will not earn you or your agents any money.

C. Survey Your Agents—If your agents won't support and actively market your trade program, it won't have a chance to get off the ground. Find out if the interest is there after your agents really understand the advantages and limitations of a trading program.

D. Forms—You will need two forms for your trading program. A letter of guarantee, stating the agreement to purchase at a specific price and date, and a worksheet showing fees, deductions, etc., will enable you to give a professional presentation to your sellers.

E. Appraisals—Select your appraiser carefully. If you elect to use someone in-house, pay him or her for the appraisal and provide as much professional training and support material as possible. If you contract with an outside appraiser, choose one who has a history of being conservative and who will provide you with the service you need.

F. Advertising—Pre-plan the marketing techniques you will use to promote your program. Design your advertising so that it can be utilized in your normal, day-to-day advertising as well as in special promotions.

By following these six steps in establishing your trade program, you can begin immediately with a program that is ready, professional, and profitable.

13-7. Designing a Program that Fits Your Needs

While I have provided you with the formats of four successful trading programs, the program you choose will have to be adjusted according to your personal circumstances. Be creative. There are no strict rules that you must follow or any particular features you must or must not have. Even in the programs I have presented you, you will have to adjust for:

A. Competition

B. Capital Available

C. Average Selling Time

D. Interest Rates

E. Cash Flow

Every community is different and each office is different. Your program must fulfill the needs of your clients, while allowing you to make a profit.

13-8. Criteria Your Trading Program Must Meet

Although there are no strict rules you must follow, history has shown that for your program to be successful, it must meet certain criteria. These criteria actually boil down to proven, successful business practices.

A. All homes involved, as well as all buyers, must be clients of your company. The success margin is slim enough without reducing it by splitting a commission.

B. The property must initially be placed on the market at a reasonable price to eliminate any stigma that might be attached to the property by buyers.

C. You must have the right to accept any offer within the last 30 days of the listing agreement prior to you purchasing the property. Knowing that you are obligated to buy his or her property at a guaranteed price, the seller may want to hold out for more until the very end. If a reasonable offer is rejected, the best buyer may have been passed up. You might want to accept an offer for less than the guaranteed amount if you feel it will be more profitable in the long run. It is an option you must have for your own protection.

D. Your program must be able to meet the needs of your clients and your salespeople. A program that only protects you will alienate buyers and sellers, not to mention your salespeople.

E. Reserve funds are necessary to prevent one failure from destroying your entire program. Consider it self-insuring against loss.

F. Your program must not only be equitable for the seller-buyer, it must be understandable to the seller-buyer. If your program is too complicated or you do not have the ability to explain it simply to your clients, buyers and sellers will be afraid of your program.

G. You, as sales manager, or the broker should present all trade offers made by your company. You are in a better position to overcome objections and soothe the seller-buyer than is the agent who is representing them.

These criteria or business practices will serve to protect you from financial loss, as well as a loss of enthusiasm on the part of your salespeople.

13-9. How to Start a Trading Program on as Little as $1,000

One of the major obstacles to developing a trading program is the capital required to implement such a service. Not only are purchase funds necessary, but funds for upkeep, interest, closing costs, and utilities must also be available if you are to purchase a property.

Actually, however, as you discovered in Section 13-5A, large sums of capital need not be required if you involve enough homes and commit all commissions initially to completing the purchase. Other means are available for reducing the amount of working capital required such as borrowing 100 percent of the funds on a short-term note, with the home as collateral; assuming a low-interest rate mortgage and securing a second mortgage for the balance; or using an equity loan. Because of the amount of business you refer to local lending institutions, and your status as a dealer rather than a residential homeowner, you can dictate the terms you need.

13-10. *Ensuring Success for Your Trading Program*

Any business or product can succeed if it contains the three ingredients of success:

A. A product or service needed by the public

B. At an affordable price

C. Presented with the right marketing techniques.

This is not an oversimplified breakdown of the formula for success. While the road to success may be easier if other ingredients are present, history has shown time and time again that a product need not be attractive, convenient, durable, or the best on the market. I can immediately think of several successful projects that met only the first three criteria such as the early models of the refrigerator, the radio, or the automobile; pet rocks, the hula-hoop, or frisbees; and it is obvious that, regardless of what the commercials claim, not *every* insurance company could possibly have the best policy, yet all are doing quite well.

If you incorporate these three ingredients into your trading program it will succeed. In fact, it cannot fail. You must, however, consider your program and the above criteria from the viewpoint of the customer, rather than your own. Is the service you're offering needed by real estate buyers and sellers, considering the terms and price they must accept to take advantage of it? Is your trading fee reasonable in the minds of your clients? Are your salespeople sold on your trade program and are they marketing it at every opportunity? If, as a buyer or seller, you cannot answer yes to every one of these questions, you must make a change in your program that will enable you to respond with a positive answer. Most great ideas that fail do so because their creator forgot to honestly evaluate his or her market and its reactions.

13-11. *Selling Your Salespeople on the Benefits of Your Trading Program*

The easiest people in the world to sell are salespeople. So, sell them! Don't take for granted the fact that, because you have put together a program, your salespeople are going to take off and run with it. Salespeople are also human, and as easy as they may be to sell, they still must be sold. Show them how your program is going to help them make more sales, more money, and beat out the competition.

Most importantly, as with any client, review the weaknesses also. Give them an opportunity to speak their objections and reservations, so you can overcome them and send your agents out with a positive, motivated attitude toward your trade program. If their fears and concerns are not voiced, they will build up to even greater obstacles and prejudices.

Regardless of the program you implement, your agents will object to:

A. Waiting for their commission
B. Possible loss of part of their commission
C. Appraisals that do not give the buyer-seller enough equity with which to work

Your presentation must address these three areas and admit to them in part. At the same time, you can show your agents that you have put together a program that protects them from these objections as much as possible and, that without the program, there would be no commission in most cases because of the buyer's need to sell before making a commitment on another home.

13-12. *Side Benefits Offered by Establishing a Trade Program*

Establishing a home-trade program offers benefits other than profits or increased sales directly resulting from the program. In many offices, these extra benefits far outweigh the program itself. For a moment, let's forget any consideration of profits or losses from properties involved in trades, and only consider the bonuses you can enjoy by employing a program for releasing buyers' equities.

13-12A. *Attraction of Additional Buyers and Sellers*

Your program can be used as a valuable marketing tool, even if the client with whom you are working is not interested in a trade himself, or if you feel confident a transaction can take place without a trade. You can show a potential listing client how buyers are more likely to purchase his home through you because of your willingness to acquire the buyer's home. Or, you can show a potential buyer how his problems will be solved when you find him a home because of your trade program, and ease his mind, even though you know his home will sell without a trade being involved.

13-12B. Overcoming Objections

Your competition has nothing on you. You also have a trade program that will help move the home.

13-12C. Keeping Your Salespeople in the Fold

With a trade program, you have eliminated another tool that a competitor can use to attract your salespeople. You are offering them as much or more sales assistance as any other office could.

13-12D. Door Openers

Your salespeople have something of importance and interest to prospective real estate buyers and sellers:

"Hi, I'm Jim Marsh, with Village Real Estate. I stopped by this morning to give you a brochure on our trade programs."

The profits, increased activity, and sales that accompany your program will be much greater than the actual profits and number of transactions derived by actual trades.

14

Introducing Your Salespeople to Financing that Closes 100% of the Time

A real estate salesperson's ability to finance his or her offers is as important as an agent's ability to get the offers. Unfortunately, most sales managers treat this final step in the selling process as one that will take care of itself. The buyers and property either qualify for the type of financing the agent chooses, or they don't. This attitude is extremely costly to both the agent and the office, since financing is the one aspect of the entire transaction that the agent can totally control, without fear of competition or indecision on the part of the buyer or seller. In today's market of tight money and high interest rates, successful sales managers must be able to bring an aggressive, creative, and knowledgeable financing attitude to their real estate office.

14-1. *Anyone Can Buy a Home, But Not Every Agent Can Finance It for Them*

This, unfortunately, is a truth that every sales manager must deal with. Everyone can, and eventually will, buy a home. And some real estate salesperson is going to earn a commission by selling it to them. The goal, of course, is to see that it is your salesperson who earns that commission. In order to accomplish this, he or she must meet certain criteria:

1. Have confidence in his or her ability to finance anyone.
2. Be familiar with all available financing avenues and outlets.
3. Be able to match buyers with the right property.
4. Keep an open mind in their financing efforts.
5. Be able to design new methods to meet buyers' needs.

With your guidance, each of your salespeople can meet these criteria. Successful financing does not require an extreme amount of intelligence, education, or experience. Your duty as a sales manager is to short-cut the learning process and increase your agents' ability to finance everyone so they do not eat up territory while they are gaining the necessary skills.

14-2. How to Encourage Your Salespeople to Use Aggressive Financing Techniques

Your first and most important hurdle to overcome in developing a staff of real estate agents that can finance anyone, is to get your salespeople to take the same aggressive attitude towards financing as they do toward listing and selling. Once the proper attitude is instilled in your agents, the mechanics of financing can be easily taught. Creating the desire and confidence within someone is a guarantee of both his or her success and yours. To succeed at any endeavor requires the vision that it is possible and the desire to fulfill that vision. Once these elements are present, a human being will work until he or she succeeds, regardless of the amount of knowledge he possesses.

Two factors limit agents' success in financing buyers. First, the majority of agents do not realize they are losing countless commissions because of inept financing techniques. Second, a good many agents believe any worthwhile buyer has enough money to make financing the home of his or her choice automatic. Both of these attitudes are shortsighted and keep the majority of real estate agents competing with each other for a few select home buyers.

14-2A. Overcoming Factor #1

If your agents don't realize how many more commissions they could be earning by employing aggressive and creative financing techniques, there is no incentive for them to work any harder than they are working now. To enlighten your staff, produce some charts and examples that demonstrate what a new approach to financing can mean to them in annual earnings. Your charts should include the following statistics:

1. The number of office transactions that failed to close within the past twelve (12) months due to financing.
2. The total number of prospects that your entire staff talked to last week, no matter how briefly, who your agents dropped because they felt the prospects couldn't be financed.
3. The number of veterans in your area.
4. The average household income in your area.
5. An estimate (taken from a brief survey) of the number of individuals who are *saving* to buy a home.
6. From a survey of one medium-sized apartment building, list the number of families that would like to buy a home if they had credit, the down payment, or could afford the monthly payment.

This chart will produce some staggering figures. Your agents will see hundreds of prospects ready to buy, simply waiting for an agent to show them how. With each statistic, you will present ideas on how your agents can earn commissions by working with these people. You should also point out a fact that most agents don't realize: *No one is actively working this market.* They are wide open and competition free.

14-2B. *Overcoming Factor #2*

One day, I was trying to find $500 for a client to use as a down payment on an FHA loan. Overhearing my attempts to raise the money, a fellow agent came over to my desk.

"Surely your buyers have $500," he exclaimed, "Anybody can lay their hands on that much money."

He honestly believed that. He had been in the upper income bracket for so long that he had forgotten what it was like to support a wife and four kids on a factory worker's income. This agent is not alone in his fantasy. Time and again, agents have expressed disbelief that a buyer didn't have funds available for a down payment. There are more people without money than people with money. Yet, since real estate sales-people have become used to doing business with people who have made up their minds to buy a home and sought out the agent, they take it for granted that everyone has saved for a down payment. To be successful, a salesperson must realize that the biggest market of buyers consists of those who literally have no money.

Suggest some financing techniques that have been used successfully in the past, in order to get your agent's creativity flowing. From your experiences and your files, give eight or ten examples of how seemingly hopeless transactions were closed solely because of the agent's financing abilities. Coupled with your chart, these examples will stimulate the attitude your salespeople must have if they are to use financing to increase their sales and their closings.

14-3. *Teaching Your Agents the Ins and Outs of Available Financing Avenues and Outlets*

You can never teach your salespeople everything concerning financing since, if they are truly creative and aggressive in this area, they will develop techniques that no one else has ever used. They must, however, be aware of the basic mechanics of each avenue of financing, and have some ideas of outlets for each before they can begin using their own imagination to make any one method work for a particular buyer. To effect this end, you must educate them concerning what you know can be done and why a particular method and source is better for a particular buyer than another.

For meetings of your entire staff, a chart is the most effective method of communicating. You should also provide each sales-person with typewritten instructions they can include in their listing book for easy access when they have a question. (Ideas on compiling a financing handbook are included later in this chapter in Section 14-6.)

At least one sales meeting each month should be dedicated to exploring the possibilities contained within a different method of financing. Once or twice a year, I even have an evening meeting just to discuss financing with my agents. As valuable as evening hours are, the time has been well spent discussing financing as is evident by the increased sales that follow. Address the not-so-obvious aspects of each method, and emphasize that small details determine the success or failure of their financing ventures.

You should be able to tell your salespeople which outlets are best in different situations, who to see, how to approach the lender, how to put the application together, and how to improve a buyer's financial picture. It is not unusual for an office to let the sales manager or a financing specialist handle the financing for the entire office. This practice costs your salespeople five, six, or more commissions each year, however, because if your agents don't know what can be done with financing, they are going to pass up prospects, mismatch properties and buyers, and appear incompetent. You also can't tell your agents how to finance a prospect and/or an offer each time they put together a transaction. If they don't follow through with each step themselves, they will not recognize the obstacles or learn to be creative in overcoming them. Only jumping in and working the transaction through allows your agents to learn to be creative.

14-4. *Financing Avenues with Local and National Outlets for All of Your Agents' Needs*

An excellent way to open up your agents' minds to creative financing is to show them the numerous methods and sources available to them for financing real estate. Once they realize that local lenders and conventional financing methods account for only a very small percentage of the available money supply, your agents will be able to broaden their thinking.

To provide your salespeople with this insight, let's take a look at developing a financing chart like the one suggested earlier. The format on page 262 will convey the message you want your agents to receive.

On the next page of your easel, draw a chart that shows the salespeople which avenues can be used with which outlets. Remind them that their outlets need not be local.

Now list the advantages and disadvantages of each financing avenue and each outlet. Give your agents some examples of when they might best use each particular type of financing. You should also explain to your salespeople in which circumstances each local outlet is best used, considering personalities, loan requirements,

---

Financing Avenues with Local and National Outlets

Avenues	*Outlets*
1. FHA 203B (Normal FHA)	1. Banks
2. VA	2. Savings and Loans
3. FHA-VA	3. Mortgage Companies
4. Farmers Home Administration	4. Finance Companies
5. 95% Insured	5. Credit Unions
6. 90% Insured	6. Pension Funds
7. Conventional Uninsured	7. Insurance Companies
8. Blanket Mortgages	8. Private Individuals
9. Package Mortgage	9. Federal Government
10. Equity Loans	10. Federal Land Bank
11. Second Mortgage	11. Mutual Funds
12. Assumption	12. Commercial Banks
13. Contract	13. Contract Sellers (Original)
14. Farm Loans	14. Sellers
15. Commercial Real Estate Loans	15. Relatives
16. Pledge (Two Types)	16. Lease Companies
17. FHA 222	
18. FHA 235	
19. FHA Multi-Unit Loans	
20. Wrap-Around Mortgages	
21. Construction Loans	
22. Balloon Payment Mortgages	
23. Purchase-Lease	
24. SBA	
25. FHA 203 (New Home Loans)	
26. VA New Home Loan	
27. Chattel Mortgages	
28. Purchase Money Mortgage (Owner Finances)	
29. Exchange	
30. Notes (Commercial or Private)	

---

etc. Discuss the quirks found in each financing avenue and how they can be used to the agent's advantage.

I also invite a different lender each month to my sales meetings to discuss his institution's requirements. Besides getting a better grasp of the standards set by the institution, my agents also have an opportunity to read the personality of the lending officer.

Places where money can be obtained:

	1	2	3	4	5	6	7	8	9	10	11	12	13	14	15	16
1	x	x	x						x							
2	x	x	x						x							
3	x	x	x						x							
4									x							
5	x	x	x													
6	x	x	x													
7	x	x		x	x			x							x	
8	x	x		x	x			x							x	
9	x				x										x	x
10	x				x			x							x	
11	x	x		x	x			x						x	x	
12	x	x	x	x	x			x						x	x	
13								x					x	x	x	
14	x	x					x	x	x	x			x		x	
15	x	x	x			x	x	x			x	x	x	x	x	
16		x					x			x				x	x	
17		x							x							
18		x							x							
19		x							x							
20	x	x				x		x				x	x	x	x	
21	x	x			x			x	x			x			x	
22	x	x				x	x	x			x	x	x	x	x	
23							x							x	x	x
24	x	x						x				x				
25	x	x	x						x							
26	x	x	x						x							
27	x			x		x		x				x	x		x	x
28														x		
29	x	x						x				x	x	x	x	
30	x			x	x		x	x				x	x	x	x	

Most importantly, impress upon your agents that a majority of financing boundaries are those they mentally confine themselves to. *If something hasn't been done in the past, it surely can't be done.* That is the attitude you must destroy and replace with a positive one! Your agents must know that if it hasn't been done before, it's a perfect way to go this time. No one has figured out why they should say no yet, so their method is likely to work. Remember, FLIP mortgages and wrap-around mortgages were developed by real estate sales-people, not lenders. We must set the pace, not the lender.

14-5. Using Financing to Generate Sales

Getting financing approval for their transaction is often the most difficult step for the real estate agent. Every commission seems to hinge on the decision of a lender. *If the financing goes through* is the contingency in the agent's mind on every offer. Because of this last, decisive step, many agents think of financing as a necessary evil, and an obstacle to overcome on their way to selling success. It is only natural then, that agents would begin to have a negative attitude towards financing, since, in their own minds, they already have the commission earned, and failure to get a loan commitment loses them that commission.

Because of these negative feelings, real estate agents fail to see the real opportunities that financing provides them. Financing should not be the only obstacle between a commission and a sales-person; it should be the factor that earns them the commission to start with. Financing can actually generate sales—sales that your people are now passing up.

Each week we have clients come to our office who have been told by other salespeople that they do not qualify for a real estate loan. When we tell them they *can* purchase a home, and that we have a home that meets their financial ability, they buy it. These buyers want *a* home, not *the* home. They buy the financing as much as or more than they buy the home.

We carry this positive attitude even one step further. Weekly, we advertise specifically for this type of prospect. Our ad addresses the very concerns these buyers have and gives them confidence that we can help them become a homeowner. Simple ads such as the ones opposite will keep your phones lit up:

FINANCING AVAILABLE: You can buy a house today, regardless of your circumstances. We have financed clients with credit problems or little or no money for down payments, buyers with moderate incomes, singles, widows, divorcees, retirees, and even clients who had filed bankruptcy. As financing experts, we have the ability and contacts to develop a financing program just for you, using over 30 different methods of real estate financing. If you want a house, not excuses, call us right now at . . .

OR

VETERANS: Did you know that your real estate eligibility did *not* run out with your other benefits? That you can buy up to a $100,000 home without a down payment or even closing costs? That you can use your eligibility more than once? That you get special consideration from the VA? That you can buy a farm or apartment building under VA? We know. Call us today for more details at . . .

OR

$500 AND AN INCOME: If you have these two ingredients, we can help with the rest and put you into this sharp, two-bedroom starter home. The owner will even pay all closing costs. If you've thought you couldn't buy a home because of the down payment, monthly payments, or your credit, call us today and we'll make you a part of the home-owning community.

OR

ANYONE CAN BUY A HOME: If the only reason you've waited to buy a home is that you don't have a down payment, or because you have a limited income, or because you do not have good credit, you need not wait any longer. Regardless of what you've been told, you can buy a home through Ajax Realty. Our professionals have the ability to get anyone financed. Stop in today or call 555-1111 and review our selection of homes and financing programs. If you have the will, Ajax Realty has the way.

OR

IF YOU'VE BEEN TOLD "NO," YOU HAVEN'T TALKED TO US! We make our living succeeding where others fail. Take five minutes, right now, and call us at . . . Our record of financing buyers proves that we can show you how to become a home owner, regardless of what others have told you.

Once the phones start ringing, though, your salespeople must be prepared to handle their new prospects. Not only must they know how to get these people financed and how to overcome their problems, but they must also present a positive attitude when the prospects calls. If your agents appear negative, you will have wasted your advertising dollars, and they will have missed out on a commission.

14-6. Compiling a Financing Handbook to Increase Your Salespeople's Success

A complete and comprehensive handbook on financing avenues, outlets, and requirements is a necessity if your salespeople are to take advantage of every opportunity presented them to earn a commission. They cannot wait until they get back to the office to confer with you on each prospect, and more than one commission has been lost because a real estate agent forgot about a particular method of financing or a criteria the buyer or home had to meet.

I first came up with the idea of a financing handbook when an agent came to me one day and said he could have sold a home we had listed except that the buyers didn't have enough down payment. He had spent two hours with them the night before, trying to find a way to come up with the funds they needed, but to no avail. When I asked him why he didn't write the offer, subject to the sellers taking a second mortgage for the amount or a note until the buyers received their tax refund in February, he admitted that the thought hadn't occurred to him. When he called his clients to suggest such an arrangement, however, they had already made an offer on another home that did not require as large a down payment. At that moment, I realized that this agent's lost commission was my fault for not preparing him to cover any problem with financing that might arise. From that time on, we had a financing handbook that every agent carried with him or her, just like the listing book.

14-6A. Selecting Material to Be Contained in Your Financing Handbook

The following is an itemized list of material you should incorporate into your handbook:

1. A listing of every avenue of financing
2. A listing of every outlet of financing, including specific lenders or lease companies, as well as those listed in general in Section 14-3 of this chapter

3. Basic requirements of each method and a brief explanation concerning when each is best used

4. A cross reference that shows the agent which types of financing can go together

5. A listing of sources and ideas for securing down payment funds

6. Point quotes, interest rates, and closing costs for each local lender or mortgage company that services your area (These must be constantly updated, of course.)

7. The phone numbers of all lenders and lease companies you are familiar with and the names of the officers your agents should talk to

8. An explanation of how to complete an offer to purchase for each method of financing

Give them ideas that will allow them to catch the ball when the buyer throws it to them. Each time you or one of your agents tries something new that works, include it in the handbook as an option for all of your agents to try.

In connection with your financing handbook, each salesperson should have a supply of applications for FHA, VA, SBA, all local lending institutions and lease companies, and FHA and VA contract sales or direct loans. While they won't need them in most cases, many times they will be working with an out-of-town buyer who must leave on the weekend and cannot make it to the lender, or they will have a situation that calls for their taking the application anyway such as SBA and FHA, or VA direct loans.

14-7. How I Financed 100% of Our Office's Offers

When I took over as sales manager of a medium-sized real estate office, sales had been steadily slipping, as had the number of salespeople. My first priority was to survey our pluses and minuses to determine where my immediate attention was needed to bring about an upsurge in the shortest possible time. What I found was that not one of the agents, even though they were experienced, was knowledgeable, creative, or aggressive with financing. The broker-owner had one of the best financing minds I've ever known, but he hadn't been able to communicate this knowledge to his salespeople.

Instead, he would work with them to close their transactions once they had an offer. With his limited time schedule, he could do no more.

I realized that if the salespeople were limited in their knowledge about financing, and their attitude was noncreative and nonaggressive, they were passing up a majority of their commissions. No wonder sales were slipping! If the buyer couldn't tell them how to finance the property, the chances were the offer wasn't going to be written. As the market got tougher, they weren't in a position to compete for the buyers' business.

It was obvious what we were going to discuss in my first sales meeting. I bought an easel and compiled charts similar to those discussed earlier in this chapter. We reviewed each avenue of financing, as well as the different outlets available. I gave them a brief rundown on each local lender, and case examples of transactions that were begun and closed by using creative financing techniques. I showed them how to get appraisals raised, use secondary markets, and combine financing methods to secure all the funds necessary to close a transaction.

The results were amazing but predictable. Within days, the salespeople were working with a clientele they never even realized could purchase a home. By the end of the first month, our office sales had doubled. Within a year, we had grown to the fourth largest office in the county. Of course, there were other factors attributing to our success, but our ability to capitalize on creative financing made everything else possible.

To ensure that every possibility was reviewed when considering financing methods, I oversaw each transaction from offer to closing. The salespeople handled their own financing, but I was familiar with every detail. When they encountered an obstacle, I knew where they had been and with what they had to work. It was important, especially during the first year, that I was able to give them a second opinion. I could bring fresh ideas to each problem, because I hadn't been concentrating on going in one particular direction.

The result was a perfect financing record on over 300 transactions. Not all, or even a majority, were secured in the first effort, but they were all closed, and that's where the commission checks are earned.

14-8. Never Assume the Obvious

One of the biggest mistakes salespeople make is to assume that one particular avenue is impossible if another avenue doesn't work, or that something is automatic. There is no magic to financing or selling success. Success comes from creativity, from work, and, most importantly, from diligently checking out each aspect of a transaction or avenue available to you.

As a financing/real estate consultant, I am understandably presented daily with some very difficult financing problems. Just recently, I assisted in the closing of a transaction that is a perfect example of not assuming the obvious, however.

The buyer had made an offer to purchase, subject to assuming the first mortgage and securing a second mortgage on his present home for the balance of the purchase price. Because of 18 percent interest rates, the buyer was unwilling to secure a permanent first mortgage, feeling that the rates would be dropping within the next few months. Since he had good credit, stable employment, and the mortgage balance he was assuming was under $10,000, the assumption seemed routine.

Even though the buyer was willing to allow the interest rate to be adjusted upward, however, the lender rejected his application on the assumption until his present home was sold! Dumbfounded, the agent asked for my help. Since I was able to analyze his needs in a fresh manner, I looked at the problem with an open mind. I was faced with two unchangeable conditions: the buyer wouldn't take out a first mortgage, and the particular lender wouldn't approve an assumption. A contract wouldn't work because a second mortgage on both properties was needed to complete the transaction.

One phone call solved the problem. I called the bank where the buyers did business and asked for a six-month equity loan, with a second mortgage on both homes as collateral, for the entire purchase price of the new home. The lender agreed and the property was closed within a week. The buyer now could sell his present home and wait for lower interest rates before securing a first mortgage.

Sounds easy, doesn't it? Actually, getting an approval *is* easy; it's being creative enough to think of the right method that's tough.

Don't allow your agents to become so complacent that they assume buyers have all the down payment money, the good credit, or the stable income they need, or that one particular method of financing is a sure thing. Assumptions leave us off-guard and we aren't prepared for problems that arise.

14-9. *Teaching Your Salespeople to Work with Lenders*

Developing a rapport with lenders is as important as developing a rapport with buyers and sellers. I don't mean you must, or even that you should, become buddies with the lenders; but rather that an agent should approach them with the same well-planned, professional technique that he or she would use with a client. After all, lending officers are human, too. They don't like overly aggressive or demanding people. On the other hand, they are going to be concerned if the agent is not confident in the parties involved or in the transaction. I have never once had a lender suggest a particular method of financing to me, at least knowingly.

Your salespeople must sell the lender, just as he or she would anybody else. The agent must be the one to plant the idea, to reassure when necessary, and to show how any difficulties can be overcome.

If I get a rejection, I want to know why, so when I go down the street to the next lender, I can have the problem corrected. If a lending officer tells me something won't work, I ask him or her if it's ever been tried. If the lender can't *prove* to me that my idea isn't productive, I push for implementation. I have closed dozens of transactions that lenders initially told me weren't possible.

To receive favors, you must grant favors. Sooner or later, you have to "put in" if you are going to continue to "take out." If you can give the lender more points, higher interest, an extra nice loan, or additional time, do. Share your business, both the easy sales and the tough ones. When you ask for a favor, you want the lender to know he or she owes you one. Spread your personal and business accounts around. Every lender in town, or as many as possible, should know that you are a customer, and can take your business elsewhere.

And *always, always* encourage your salespeople to ask why!

Don't let them become obnoxious, but do let them be inquisitive. They will only *learn* after they know *why* a decision was made. They may also find that there is no answer to their "why?" in which case they will have earned a commission check!

Index